America:
Final Destination

Veronika Paul

Avid Readers Publishing Group
Lakewood, California

The opinions expressed in this manuscript are those of the author and do not represent the thoughts or opinions of the publisher. The author warrants and represents that she has the legal right to publish or owns all material in this book. If you find a discrepancy, contact the publisher at www.avidreaderspg.com.

America: Final Destination

All Rights Reserved

Copyright © July, 2011 Veronika Paul
Registration Number TXu 1-753-387

This book may not be transmitted, reproduced, or stored in part or in whole by any means without the express written consent of the publisher except for brief quotations in articles and reviews.

Avid Readers Publishing Group

http://www.avidreaderspg.com

ISBN-13: 978-1-61286-050-3

Printed in the United States

Introduction

This is the true story of my journey from Paraguay, south America to California on a 125 cc Honda Motorcycle in 1987. I love to travel, explore and learn about other cultures, their tradition and blend in. The unknown mystery makes life interesting as well challenging. As a child I envied the nomadic life of the sheep herder, always on the move and home is everywhere. My dream became to travel the world like Marco Polo. I grew up in Germany and was mostly a loner, a dreamer and loved to read. When I shared with people my dream, they told me, you need to marry a rich man. I refused and became determined to earn my own money and pursue my dream.

In 1985 I moved to Paraguay to live and travel more. My American friends Ray and Nancy stayed in touch with me to visit them in California. Instead of flying I chose to drive my motorcycle. I visited embassies inquiring about visas and information about their country.

There were none. No travel guide books to buy. Only America required a visa. The American embassy cautioned me not to drive through Nicaragua, due to the Guerilla war. They urged me to take the banana boat from Lima to America. I just nodded. I did get a map from the Automobile Club in Asuncion showing the major roads. After months of planning and dreaming I realized it would be a shot in the dark. My close friends cautioned me of the danger and risk to travel alone as a woman in south America off the beaten path. It didn't discourage me. I shook hands with death a few times and told him not yet. My travel and explorer fever was stronger. I followed my hearts desire. I planned two months of travel hopefully to arrive in April, just in time for Nancy's vacation. Instead it took me four and a half months. I realized that in south America time is meaningless. You travel when the weather permits. Mother nature is in charge, not you. You get there when she says so.

In 2008 after my second divorce. My best friend Jim and I vacationed in Maui, Hawaii. We visited Ray and Nancy at their home. It was a happy reunion after many years. We had a wonderful time and I promised to write my travel story. It took three years to complete. Special thanks to my best friend Jim. He is a musician, poet and writer. He supported and encouraged my writing. He gave me suggestions about the structure of my book. Tireless he read, reviewed and edited. English is my second language. He helped to make this book possible.

I want to thank as well my friends in Paraguay for their friendship and caring. I like to thank the people and friends I met during my trip. To help me in one way or other. With some I came very close and it was hard to leave. Captain Uribe and his ship crew, his wife Dorthy for taking in Jaco. In Costa Rica Juan Villalobos with family, wife Rita, sisters Nelly, Sereneida, Elieth, Albero and his family. Mariano from Guatemala, Dr. Carlos his wife Ariciela and sister Martha, husband Augustine with family. In America Mr. Rat and the bikers. Nancy and Ray Steven. I have not forgotten you. A special thank you to all my friends and my parents in Germany. Some are no longer here on this earth, but the memories are. Remember Life is a journey not a destination.

Thank you to Eric Patterson from Avid Readers. He is a fun and easy to work with. I shared my vision of the lay out of my book and asked for his professional opinion. It blew me away.

Map of Travel

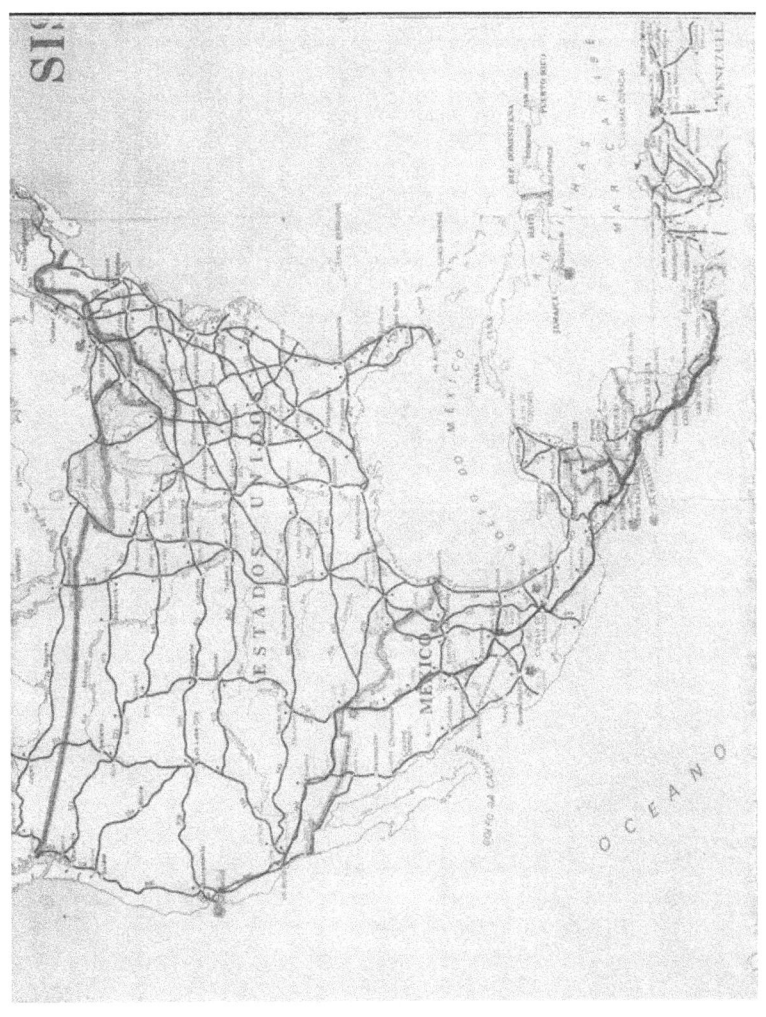

Map of Travel

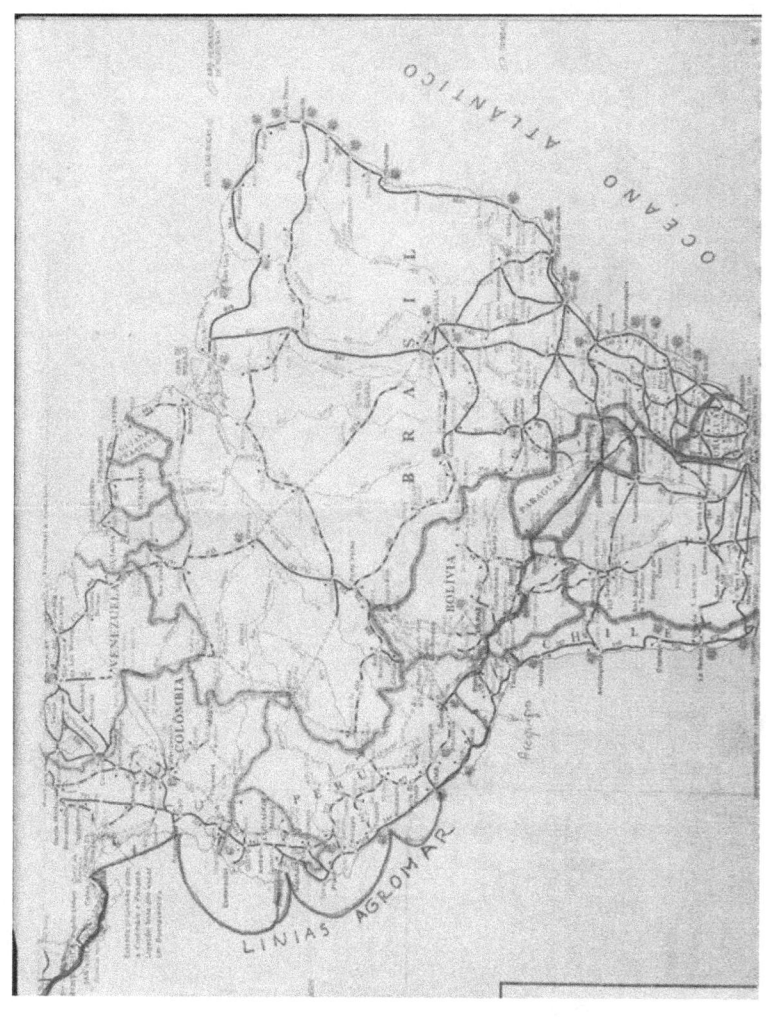

GERMANY

Born in Stuttgart in 1960 and grew up in a suburb 15kilometer outside of the city, in Gerlingen. A valley surrounded with hills on one side. It used to be a cow town. We lived on the outskirts of the quiet town overlooking open spaces and fields. We lived in a duplex. My father owned his house. His parents owned the other house. My father is the oldest son, his two younger brothers live in the parents house and one brothers lives in America. As I grew up more and more houses got built around us. We always walked a lot. My father bought a little black car, a Prince. On Sundays the whole family, my parents, our grandma, my brother and I went on daytrips. I spent a lot of time with my grandma since both of my parents worked. Soon we outgrew the little black Prince. My father bought a medium green Prince. Now we were able to take longer and more extensive trips. Visiting extensive family and exploring Germany. There were only a few highways so we traveled mostly country roads and visiting Friends of Nature houses (Naturfreunde Haus) and went on hikes there. Every weekend we were on the go, except weekends we harvested fruits or cut and stacked wood for wintertime for heating our home. We always had tenants renting in our home. They preferred coal. Downstairs lived a single Lady for a long time then followed an Italian family. Upstairs lived a single lady for a long time and then a Greek couple. It was the early seventies. We learned a lot about their customs and culture. One summer we visited my mom's brother in northern Germany in Flensburg. We hardly understood them due to our dialect. From there we visited

Denmark. We rented a house for weeks and ate fresh fish everyday. Every summer and spring we went on vacation to Austria, Switzerland, Tirol and northern Italy.

    In 1972 my grandma died. My uncle came from America. Inviting me to come to visit them in Chicago, Illinois. I refused remembering my grandma telling me how boring their life style was. She was alone all day. The parents worked and the kids were in school until late in the afternoon. She had to make her own lunch everyday. The area is flat like a pancake. She always looked forward to coming home. So did I, because she already had a TV, a toaster and made popcorn. We watched TV until midnight and then had a midnight snack. A warm toast. She was very caring. In the sixties very few Germans had a TV. I remember coming home from school one day and watching on TV. People walking on the moon. There were many reasons I stayed with my grandma. She also brought back real chewing gum. My parents hated it, because after chewing them we glued them under the table or bed. I wasn't excited to go to America, besides I discovered a pony horse farm. It was a rental to the public. I love horses and started to get involved. My uncle disappointed took my brother instead. He was suppose to stay six weeks, but returned two weeks early. He got sick and the doctors couldn't find the cause of sickness. He spent months in and out of the hospital in Stuttgart. Finally they diagnosed him with rheumatoid. Later he was sent to a specialty clinic in Garmish Partenkirchen a very beautiful town in Bavaria on the border Czech Republic. My mom and I spent my school vacation there to visit my brother daily and we explored the area.

    We were sent as well with other kids twice to wellness vacations in winter. Once to the island of Syllt the other winter to the island Amrum to strengthen our immune system in the north sea.

At the age of six I was sent to a wellness vacation with other kids to Allgaeu in Bavaria. I learned there not to copying other kids mischief. I got caught copping them and sent to detention. I didn't like that and promised myself to just go my own way. We had a good a good life. well cared by our parents. They wanted us to have a better life. Both my parents grew up in world war two.

After my grandmas death, one February my father said. He is going on a business trip, but he wouldn't say where. For one week. The day of his arrival. We received a telegram stating. He will return a week later. It was a cold snowy winter in Germany. When our father returned. We were in shock. He was dark browned tanned. Now he told us. He vacationed two or three weeks on the canary islands sunbathing everyday. While we froze in Germany. He became the talk of the town. We envied him. The next year he took our mom, while we had to be with our unflavored grandma from my mom's side. She was extremely strict. She didn't like me going to the horse stables everyday. I didn't care and went anyhow. After my fathers grandmas death, this became my second home and interest. I and other girls of my age and teenagers hung out there on a regular basis. We helped with the horses feeding, caring, renting the horses to the public and collecting the money. In exchange we got free pony/horse rides. Right after school I went home for lunch and changed my clothes. I did my homework before going to bed. Overtime we were allowed to attended or better said we were handling the entire horse rental, attending church functions or fundraisers. We walked the ponies for the kids, were the driver of the pony carriages. We came around. The owners treated us like their extended family. He taught us a lot. We got riding lessons. We were his right hand.

My parents didn't like me to go there, because it was to close to a village of low in come housing. My father warned me. Don't come home pregnant. We won't rise your single child. I told him. I am not interested in the boys only the horses. My only interest and traveling.

Christmas eve 1976. We came from church. Wee are used to see presents under the tree, there were none. I asked my father with his dry humor and not talkative. Where are our presents? He was quiet than he finally answers. You won't like it. It is only a envelope. A envelope, I said. Where? Please let me see it. My father handed me a envelope, than one for my mom and my brother followed. Curious I opened it first. A airline ticket, everybody got a ticket. I take a closer look December 31 1976 to Tenerife the Canary islands for two weeks. I was so happy. Finally we would go to the to the islands. Where my father, my parents went in winter and returned dark brown. We had a great time, warm weather, sun and beaches.

In the summer of 1977, my last school year, we planned to drive to Yugoslavia. A Yugoslavian schoolmate taught me some basic words. My father had bought a new VW Passat. The two of us drove a 1 000km to the Adriatic sea in Croatia to find a place to stay. My mother followed later by train due to illness. We found a small family run motel close to Omish/ Split. We became friends with the family. For years my parents went every summer until the war started.

In august 1977 I started a Pastry cook apprentice ship/trade school in Stuttgart for three years. It was a big change in my life. I had to get up every morning at 3:45 the latest at four to catch the strassenbahn -streetcar to be at six in the morning at the bakery/pastry/coffee shop Walter Nast. Then standing for eight hours on tile floors. One day a week we had Trade school. It was a relief it started at eight in the morning and every second week we had a half a day from noon field knowledge. That was fun. We made fresh candy, pralines little chocolate, etc or just experiments. Most is now industrialized due to cost. My dream was to travel the world as Pastry cook. Our teacher predicted that most of us will not stay in the profession. Artists don't get paid well and a shift in the industry. Cruise ships are declining under German flag. In ten years he will be teaching the knowledge of machines instead of field knowledge. That took the air out of me. Despite the change I was determined to travel the world. Hotels still need Pastry cooks-Patisserie. He told us the more famous the hotels, the lower the pay for the assistants. Some even volunteer just to learn from the gourmet chefs and have their name on their resume. As a apprentice we got only two weeks vacation a year. One year I went to he stud farm Marbach by the creek lauter. A horse riding vacation. The next year to France coast ST. Malo for wind surfing.

    Close to my exit exam I volunteered for a week at the five star hotel Zeppelin in Stuttgart. It was a different world. The hours are from nine in the morning till three in the afternoon, then off. Start again at six till ten at night. The employees were very nice and I was eager to learn. I loved it there. It was a slow summer season, if there was nothing to do for the confectionery/ patisserie I went to the kitchen looking the cooks over their shoulder. They just smiled and explained their cooking. I learned a lot and got sometimes a bite to taste.

    In September 1980 I got hired at the Castle Hotel Kronberg, in Taunus the former summer residence from the queen of England. I had a furnished room in a real stone tower. In a circle the steps led up to my room. I was filled with of joy which didn't last long. My boss a single middle aged man was critizing my work all the time. Why? Perhaps my cookies were nicer and smaller. I reminded him confectioner/patisserie means small, nice and perfect. This is a four star hotel. A slice of cake was five marks. He got more tolerant.

One day the kitchen chef talked to me privately. We have a big important party coming up. He is a regular customer, but had been unhappy the last time. He gives us one more chance. Could you make a special desserts? Of course I replied happy. I suggested pralines and fine tea cookies. He was happy. To keep the peace with my boss I came in at six in the morning with the cooks making the pralines and the fine tea cookies on my own time. My boss didn't like it, but I had the kitchen chefs approval. The days until the party were very intense with preparation. Finally the night of the party came. We made a dessert with different fresh fruits. Each fruit was pureed separately and poured in a circle like spikes on a wheel. It was quite colorful. I filled a silver tray with assorted pralines and assorted tea cookies the kitchen chef loved my pralines with a touch of liquor. He asked me after the guests dinner to serve them to the party guests in the library now. I looked forward to it. The hint came I changed into a clean white shirt and took off with my tray. It was after ten o'clock at night overtime for me. The library was filled with happy chatting people. I walked around offering my goodies. Many men told me, we are full or we just had dinner. I was devastated and disappointed. Did I make all that for nothing? I wondered. When I came around the second time some tasted them and were delighted and asked me to have some sent to his room. I did. Close to midnight only a handful of men were here. I was tired from working and running back and forth filling my tray, but I did one last round offering my desserts. The men sat talking in a circle I offered my tray. He chased me away, but one man says smiling. Show me what you have and explain every single one. I was only 20 years old. I felt great describing each cookie and each praline. He tasted them and loved them. While the others talked business. The friendly man asked me about my future and my goals. Delighted I told him. I want to travel the world. The hostess butted in and said. Then you have to marry a rich man. I said, I want to earn my own money and be independent. The hostess was negative. The friendly man responded look how we got started after the war. We had nothing and look at us today. There was a moment of silence. I could feel and tell everyone was wealthy and well off. It felt so good to get his support, took a deep breath and asked the hostess. If he would like to take some dessert home for his family, his wife and children. He told me to pack a box to go.

The next day I got critized from everyone especially my boss. How could you ask him to take dessert home? How do you know he his married and have a wife and children? I smiled and brushed them off, thanking for their advice. It's over get off my back. A few days later the hotel manager called me to his office. He told me the party was saved. Shared his surprise that the client took dessert home. That never happened before and we retain him as a client. I was happy with him, but my work relationship got worse tense. I left shortly after as well the kitchen chef. Back to Stuttgart.

In spring of 1981 I went on a bus tour to Greece. On the way home we stopped in St. Wolfgang, Austria. I got into a conversation with a cook and he offered me a job. A few days later I returned to meet with the restaurant owners. I could start right away as pastry cook and salad post. I went home to tell my parents and to pack a few belongings. My father was delighted. His name is Wolfgang, I will be working in St. Wolfgang at the hotel /restaurant Peter for the summer season. I loved it there. It as a good environment and very pretty. On my days off I took daytrips to the surrounding area. I didn't own a car. We got lots of tour busses coming for lunch. It was very busy and crazy, but we worked hand in hand and kept our humor. Summer went by fast back to Stuttgart. I was offered a position in a ski resort for the winter season in Austria, but I couldn't see myself making beds and cleaning all day. Instead I stayed in Stuttgart and became a Taxi driver. One day I ran into an old friend Beate. We talked. What are you doing tonight? She invited me to go with her to the American base. She had a date and I tagged along. We went to the movies and to the bar. She had lived a few years in America and spoke fluent English while I struggled. However we made it a habit to hang out with the GI's. It was fun trying to refresh my school English and parting. One day her father was lecturing her to work more and stop the excuses. Curious I asked, what are you doing and how much are you get paid? He answered, its sales and only commission based. I was interested, he thought this is not for me. I kept bugging him. One day he gave in. they needed more people. It was the early spring of 1982. I was excited but he kept saying. He doesn't want to loose our friendship. Why? I questioned. We would be only working for the same company. I never understood what he meant. Excited I made an appointment with the boss in his beautiful house in the black forest. He wasn't convinced I would last, hut he gave me a two week trial. Beate's father had to train me. We met one Friday morning. We went to five companies then we had lunch. That's it now you are on your own. Nervous I asked for some advice. He gave me some instruction and went home. That was it. I was speechless. It wasn't easy, but the pay potential kept me motivated. Finally I could realize my dream. In one week with less hours I made more money than working as Pastry cook in a month. Setting my own hours. I surprised everybody. From now on I made good money and saved and traveled. That year to Hungary, Italy and made a new friend Nancy. We became good buddies and she knew how to party as well spoke fluent English. Every weekend we hung out with American GI's and a few of her friends.

America: Final Destination

In 1983 I went to Great Britain and Ireland for three week camping Bus tour. A month later on six week Bus camping tour in America. From New York through the south to Anaheim in Los Angeles up to San Francisco through the north to Niagara Falls with Contikki tours for young people from around the world. In Niagara falls I split and visited friends in Toronto, Ottawa and Montreal in Canada for a week. By bus through the beautiful state of New York to the city. My boss wasn't to happy about my long vacations, but happy when I returned.

In spring of 1984 I went on a luxurious two week bus tour in South Africa. The only safe way to travel there. Met in Cape town with a German family from a previous trip. They lived there since the fifties, he used to work for Bosch. We traveled to the table mountain overlooking the beautiful city. The next day on a day tour to the cape of good hope I met Nancy and Raymond Stevens from California. We stayed in touch.

That summer I planned to buy a one year old 944 Porsche for a good price from a factory worker, but my uncle, my fathers youngest brother living next door, talked me out of it. He says the insurance would kill me. I was 24 years old. I gave in to him and traveled instead to Asia for the summer for only 10 weeks. I thought my boss would get a heart attack when I told him. I can't promise you work when you come back he warned me. I took a chance and went to the Maldives islands, visiting a friend in Singapore, Malaysia, Sumatra(Indonesia) Hong Kong, Korea, Taiwan and Thailand. On my own and located my friend in Seoul, Korea and hiked the mountain in chew islands with Korean students.

After my return my boss awaited me with open arms. A few workers fell ill. My coworker Mr. Mulder was in the hospital with a minor heart attack. The boss had put us together we were his reliable team. We always got the out of town districts. We left Monday and returned Friday afternoon. Some people thought we were sister and brother or father and daughter. We laughed. No we just work together. Every Monday morning we met Mr. Mulder would ask before taking off. How was your weekend? Where did you go? He knew every weekend I was hanging out with my friends and the American GI's. We party at night and the next day we went sightseeing and were their tour guide, educated them of our German culture and food. We always had a good time. Mr. Mulder enjoyed hearing my stories. He was from Holland and he was amazed from my energy. Always on the go.

My father commented. You work six months and vacation six months. How do you do that? I told him. I pay my small rent and don't ask you for any money so don't worry. I told him I wanted to buy a condo. He told me not to. You have a house so instead I traveled.

In spring of 1985 I planned to go to Tahiti, Australia and New Zealand. Then I saw an ad in the paper. Invest and live in Paradise. I called. Where is it? South America, Paraguay I associate that with the jungle. They have a tourist tour coming up. I was curious and interested to go. In a small group we traveled to Rio de Janeiro and Foz de Iguazu the big waterfalls in Brazil. Toured Paraguay by bus and flew in a small airplane to the Chaco in the north to see the Amish people. I loved it. Brought a young Amazon parrot back to Germany. My parents thought I lost my mind.

My boss was telling me, he is retiring soon and that I better get along his son of my age. He knew we had our differences. I got a call from a developer. He was planning a new village within the German colony in Paraguay. Wondering if I am interested to check it out? It was on a short notice I returned with a small group including a local architect to Paraguay. We toured the planned site. Far from the asphalt road in the country a few single homes in the distance. We drove here on a dirt road. Here they offered me a future job as pastry cook for their planned village bakery. I love the country I agreed, but didn't wanted to wait till it is built. Unhappy discontent with my work and German politics I asked locals, how easy is it to immigrate here. It's easy. My friends in Germany weren't to happy. About my decision I had a couple good GI friends interested in a serious relationship and wanting to get married I told them upfront I want out of Germany and I didn't want to get married. I felt the army has to many rules just like a communist world. My good friend Captain Charles wanted to retire from the army and live in Germany, but I wanted out of Germany. I was upfront with him to avoid hurting his feeling. Bad timing, he was a really nice guy. All my friends were unhappy, but I followed my guts and left in summer of 1985 in Germany.

My dad and mom on her 60th birthday
on a cruise in May, 1989.

PARAGUAY

We arrive in Paraguay in the middle of winter. Cold nights wet and humid there were no heaters. For a short time I stayed with new friends. Then with the family Metzger. They invited me to stay with them. Onthe cold days and nights we sat in the warm kitchen with their wood burning stove and drinking hot Yerba tea. This is a tradition. The tea is served in a small cup half filled with yerba mate and then hot water poured over. It gets passed around sucking on a metal straw. In summertime it gets served with cold water. That's the social time with family and friends. It was a good time. We explored the colony by tractor and on horse back. They were very good to me, but I wanted to bake and be on my own feet. We stayed friends.

I moved into an older vacant house in the country of the German colony. It was a rough beginning.The big kitchen had an old woodstove I used for baking. It had a solid wooden table and matching benches and two large rooms. An out house and water I had to pull with a bucket from a quell. In winter Itook only sponge baths with ice cold water. At lunchtime it got warmer and I washed my clothes by hand and hung them on the fence. In one or two hours later they were dry. A month later I bought a used two story gas pizza oven. Now I could bake larger quantities and sell my baked baked goods on foot at the fewlocal general stores. Soon I bought a young horse and took in an old abonded dog. I tamed the young fill and let her carry the pastries with a shoulder bag. It was a rough beginning. All the German farmer baked their own bread and cakes hardly bought any in a store. They said it will change down the road and the locals have not much money and I didn't speak Spanish. The colonists told me the locals the Paraguayans like big pieces and cheap. It wasn't easy. I experimented to find their liking of pastries.

Females often told me, its not good to live alone, I should have a companion. I always said. I have my parrot, a dog and a horse. They meant a male or a child. I just shook my head I don't need extra headaches.

So there was always rumor going on about me. I was always in trouble. A few told me seriously. Go home so long you have money. You won't make it. You won't see the sun. I thanked them for their advice. I didn't want to return to Germany. My friend would laugh about me and would say. I knew you wouldn't make it. I decided to stay and move ahead. I had bought a used motorcycle but didn't know how to drive the mechanics told me its easy. Gave me a two minutes instruction. On pavement I did good, but I kissed many times the sand road. Then it constantly broke down and I spent a lot of time at the mechanic. Through another German family I bought a newer motorcycle a Brazilian 125 Honda. I sold the old bike back to the mechanic. Now I was independent and Jaco and I traveled. My father came to visit. I picked him up at the airport and took him to the German butcher in Asuncion for lunch. He liked their good sausages. We came to the colony he stayed at the only hotel close to my house. May be a 100meters away.

My father came over to see me after settling in his room. At the covered front porch he stopped. Oh my god, you live like a hunter. I am so glad I didn't bring your mother. She would a turned around on her heels and left. He toured the house and couldn't believe I had no mattress for my bed of doubled stacked pellets. He got to know several German immigrants and asked one family to deliver a mattress for me. I didn't wanted to carry a cotton mattress from the asphalt road to my house in the heat. It is a long walk. We traveled a lot. He felt like back in the fifties in Germany. We visited friends and the family Metzger. We got along very well and in the conversation. It came out that Metzger's father lived down the street where my father grew up in their home town Korntal. We laughed so hard and long. Here my father travels half around the world to meet his former neighbors. My father loved it here and considered moving here, but my mom wouldn't. He got a nickname "El Papa," he was proud of it. We visited as well the waterfalls in Iguazu in Brazil and my father insisted to buy me to motorcycle helmet and use it all the time. I moved to town Villaricca. I learned a little Spanish since I mostly sold to the locals. I was a breath of fresh air to them, because I sold by piece not by weight and it was very fresh. The Paraguayans loved my daily fresh baked goods. Cakes, pies, cookies, always something different. I learned slowly Spanish Going on foot door to door and the bus terminal, this became very popular among business people. I came in the morning baked at lunchtime and sold it the same afternoon. I knew what time the business owners eat or have their yerba tea break. They know me for the freshness, customer service. We are like a big family, if I had leftovers I gave it to my neighbor.

It was a big change to have neighbors so close, but now I could walk in minutes to the market to sell and in the afternoon. I started to take Taek-won-do classes for self defense. Men started to respect me. My business grew and then I got sick with Hepatitis. The doctor told me to go home and rest, but I drove instead to the German colony to see friends. The doc saw me driving on the dirt roads and scolded me out.

It's too dangerous, your liver could burst. It was a very hot summer and friends loaned me German books to read. I slept a lot and dreamed. To travel in Papillion's footsteps through south America.

My mom and her friend Renate came to visit. We met in Rio de Janeiro, Brazil. We did all the tourist sights, samba, the famous barbeque and slowly traveled to Paraguay. Visiting many sights. My mom didn't like how I lived. I rented one wing of a big Brick home in a L shape. I had three rooms, big bathroom, indoor shower and toilet. A big deal here. Next to me, works and lives an older gentleman running a printer shop, in one room. He has the corner, next to him was a shoe repair business. We share the same yard, but they use an outhouse and outdoor shower. Every month the shoemaker bickers about the electric bill. There is only one meter for the house. We have several trees in the yard. Jaco spent most of his time there, when I do my rounds. The neighbors are always complaining about Jaco, mostly that he picks on the fruits and drops them on the ground. When I am home, he spends time indoors sitting on a wooden folding chair. To rest or getting his food and water and give me company, while I baked. He tells me the news of his day and I tell him mine. All my neighbors are very nosy. At times it is good, if an occasional visitor came they leave a message with the printer.

To cook we had to light charcoal in a little free standing stove and wash the dishes outside in a big bowl. However by now I had a indoor toilet and shower. She said I just live like the locals so primitive and could never get over it. I protested. At night we would sit outside and look at the stars. We visited often with friends and always sitting outside enjoying the cool breeze. I asked her. Do you like my TV pointing at the stars. We are footloose and fancy free. She enjoyed her stay, but as well glad to go home. This lifestyle is not for her. We all laughed and had another glass wine.

I live there for a good year and it felt I lived here all my life. I was so well adjusted and known everywhere with Jaco and my bike. The locals called me Torta, because I couldn't roll the r like the Spanish do. I sold my cookies and cakes from Asuncion to stroessner (cuidad del Este) and in the back country. One day on my route walking in town selling door to door and at the bus terminal to the travelers. I got the news a friend from America called me. We were looking for you. I saw Eddy my former landlord and selling bus tickets. She told me my friend called a few days ago and will be calling again. Where have you been? I told her I travel to Brazil to buy merchandise and resell it in Argentina My friends reminded me. Don't forget to bring Jaco. The custom and police always search the bus on the way to Buenos Aires and no longer harassed us. They always smiled and let us go. The day came and I waited at the bus terminal for Ray to call. All the young street vendors gathered around me and waiting for the call. Everybody knows everybody. The phone rings Eddy picks up the phone and hands me the receiver through the open window. Hello this is Raymond. How are you? Fine I say. You are sure hard to get a hold of. Where have you been? I am somewhere between Sao Paulo and Buenos Aires buying and selling goods. Raymond asks when are you coming to visit us? I don't know, I have no plans. Ray gets impatient and says. For three years you promised to visit. I will look into how much airfare is and call you back. It is much more expensive from Paraguay then from Germany to fly to San Francisco, I said. We promised to stay in touch. I checked the airfares and then consulted with my wallet. If I fly to San Francisco and back and stay for a month I would return broke. Didn't like that idea. For a couple weeks different options ran through my head. Why not travel over land by bus? I gave that more thought. Traveling in crowded busses and run into problems like parrots are not allowed on a bus.

What should I do with my motorcycle? Is it safe to leave it? There are good chances it get stolen. Why not just drive and be independent and be free. Summer is coming a slow time for everybody. We are just getting by. A good time to go on vacation.

    I have basic furniture, clothes, so it didn't take long to pack, deep in my thoughts I heard a knocking on my door, curiously I went to the door. My friend Leske from the German colony. What a surprise. Come on in, I offered him. Where have you been? He didn't answer, just put his head down. Didn't you get our messages for the new years party?? I asked frustrated him! Leske says I have been busy, fixing my parents place. Why are you here now? I ask angrily? I came to town to buy some tools and see you. Really, I answer sarcastically. So what are you up to? Now I smile, I say excited. I am leaving tomorrow for a trip north. He looked shocked, asked depressed, why are you leaving me? You have a good business going, you are well known, changing his voice he says, you can't leave me. I look him in his eyes, this is my life and I do, what I want to do. In shock he says, our friendship just begun, it just ended, I completed his sentence. Would you like to give me a hand? Instead of standing around. Waiting for an answer. He was marbleized like an statue, stuttering he goes, I thought you were joking with your trip. Apparently, I reply you see I wasn't. You don't care about me. We call you and you don't answer. I haven't seen you in weeks. You come when it is convenient for you. You don't care. I continue packing. He tells me he has to go shopping. I just guide him to the door. I will be back he says. I close the door behind him. Did I tell him the truth and he couldn't handle it? I doubt he comes back. I continued packing, I am an expert, I moved so many times. I ran to the market to hire two horse carriages taxis and extra help to help load my big free standing Gas Pizza oven. The men stood around debatting how to load it. That's when leske shows up. Surprised to see him again, I say in humor, you came at the right time, we needed an extra hand. He was not excited. Did I blow his bluff?? Everything was loaded, glass vitrine, oven, bed, free standing closet, etc. I gave the men the address to unload the furniture. Ramona, Reynaldo and their three kids have a big house in downtown. In their big backyard they have a storage house, but our hangout is at Ramona's Sister Roswitha. She lives only a block away with her husband Julian their son and later his wife and a dozen little Yorkshire dogs. That is her passion Their home is smaller, but cozy. The sisters are very close and are together daily. On the end of my route I stopped in. We are best friends and we laughed a lot and shared our happiness and sadness together. Her husband Julian is a Lawyer and secretary to the Cornel of the military. Ramona's husband is a lawyer as well and travels a lot. She offered to store my belongings. Both families are well respected here. They supported my trip, but unhappily at the same time of me leaving. We will miss you and I will miss them. It wasn't a secret that I was treated like their daughter. Ramona was always happy, cheerful. She waited for us, made already room for my belongings. Everybody from the family helped to unload and store. First the big oven, then the rest. As we passed in the hallway, we told jokes. I overheard Leske whining to Reynaldo, telling her not to leave. Don't let her go on that trip. At the first opportunity, Reynaldo saw me, he turns to me, Poncho (Parrot) Leske will be very unhappy after you leave. What is Pancho Leske going to do? We all laughed so hard. At the next passing, when I was face to face with him I said triumphantly. Pancho Leske has to stay with his parents and take care of them. That's why he returned from Germany. He gave me a nasty look and got quiet and walked away. Ramona was amused about our conversation and understood very well. We stored the last piece away soaked to the bone from the sweat, catching our breath from working. Ready for water and refreshments Ramona brought. She asked curiously and looking around. Where did Pancho Leske go? We all look around and he is gone. He doesn't care about me. Haven't seen him in weeks. Just forget about him, he is not worth crying for. We wrapped up the afternoon, saying good-bye. It was very hard, to leave my best friends. We have so many good times and memories together. I promised to stay in touch. I stayed the last night with grandpa Libby Schade at their small house at the end of town. He taught me a lot. As a young child he came with his parents to Paraguay, but grew up in Argentina in the country learning the Indian language" Guarani" He speaks that better than Spanish. For his advanced age he is in good health, tall and skinny. He had a hard life, smoking his pipe daily and has still the child like look. He loves to tease his Paraguayan wife. She is smaller, a little curvy. A good housewife always in good mood, laughing. We had a delightful evening. Grandpa asked me again, in quizzes how to read the sun for directions, north, south, east and west. The sun tells you as well the time. Giving me directions like 10 blocks north, 2 blocks east. Where is it? We had fun, laughing. I was very excited for this trip, the unknown adventure, without a virtually map. Grandpa reminded me several times be very careful. Always have enough water, canned tuna with you. I promised to watch out. We both were excited and on the same hand very sad, due for me leaving. My young friends have already left to Germany or France. I would been here alone. We looked each other in the eyes. We will miss each other very much. In the morning, I loaded my bike. It looked like a overloaded donkey from Spain. I had a tiny stove, a cooler for my German chocolate, extra shoes, clothes, Jaco's pet carrier, dry food and lots of water, lemons. Grandpa gave me a few last advises, and a hearty hand shake. Be careful and stay in touch. Only a handful of friends knew of my destination. I swung on my bike, drove away with mixed feelings, happy and sad. Today I drove only to Asuncion along the road bus driver s honked at me. They all knew me and recognized my bike with jaco on the handlebar. Hausners from my hometown had migrated here a year ago with two teenagers, a few big dogs" Leonberger." The dogs didn't care for the heat, but the family did, just like me. They love the city life, for me it is to busy. A rat race. Today I was running around to see a couple friends, Gilberto and his wife, my taek-won-do teacher. Rudy, my banker. He deals with overseas investors. They invest in Jojoba, cattle's in northern Paraguay. He is very busy especially when his clients come to visit. They have high expectations and want to hear numbers. See the cattle ranches in the Chaco in northern Paraguay. It is a drier climate ideal for cattle's, but water is often a challenge. Rudy envied me for my trip. You have the money to take a vacation, he didn't reply. I will drop a line from time to time. Now to the post office to send a letter to my parents, telling them just now of my planned trip. I will be writing postcards to stay in touch and to keep them from worrying. Grandpa Schade has your address for Emergencies. Only Renate a close friend to my parents knew. She supported my trip and promised to send maps. I haven't received anything, they must have gotten delayed in the mail. I didn't want to wait. I thanked family Hausners for everything. Everybody tells me to be careful.

  January 31st today the first day of my of trip to the north. Originally I had planned to drive to Patagonia first, but that is a long trip and even the summers are cold there. Forget that, so I plan to drive to San Francisco and from there to Alaska. I was very exited and so was Jaco my co pilot. Leaving the hustling, bustling city of Asuncion. The sky was cloudy, it rained last night. I was driving and day dreaming, quickly, thinking finally to be on my trip. Jaco and I are excited, let the adventures begin. Traveling on the new asphalt roads are very boring. Just a straight road as far the eye can see. That's why the locals drive at night. The same scenery for hours. The road is built high to avoid floods. It creates lakes on both sides with hundreds of different water birds. It is a breathtaking view. Jaco was sitting on the handlebar with his wings spread open like an airplane. An sparkle in his eyes showing his happiness. A man in green clothes walking the street came in sight, as I came closer I saw a rifle hanging over his shoulder followed by two big hunting dogs. I felt uncomfortable after all the stories I heard and made a big loop around him. He didn't pay attention to us.

The more north we drove the drier it got. The Chaco is known as a desert dry heat, low rainfall, scrubs, and bushes. This climate is ideal for cattle. The white breed from India used to the heat does well here.

Less bugs means less medication for the cattle, but water is always a problem. The Chaco is sparsely populated. Mostly military resides here. The sun had come out and it got warmer.

In the afternoon the asphalt ended. A sign reads 50 km to Loma Plata/Filadelpia, the Mennonite colonies.

These are the modern Amish. Horrified I looked at the wet clay road. Took a deep breath, the sliding and skating begun. It was a challenge with all my luggage. Consequently we kissed the road several times, I was struggling to get the bike on his wheels again. The road got wetter and I fell again. I lifted the bike half way up, the back tire slide again. It's all the luggage pulling it down, the gas leaking out of the tank. I am frustrated to the fullest. Jaco we have to get to drier ground, it is to bad you can't help. I pulled and pulled on the front tire wading in red sticky clay. Jaco sat nervous on my shoulder supervising me. Soaked in sweat I succeeded. Soon the clay road turned into sandy roads, which is easier to drive. I wished I had less luggage I would be able to drive faster. I prayed to make it to town before dawn. There are no street lights here. The road became wide. I had come to a big intersection and I stopped, which way? Exhausted I sat on my bike confused looking around. Seeing only flat scenery and four different roads. To my luck a bike with a young boy crossed our way. I flagged him down. He offered to guide us to town after he noticed we are not from the colony. He drove like he wason fire and I had difficulties to following him. Kindly he waited on us, when we got out of sight. Night was coming and we were still driving. I was of the end of my rope, exhausted from driving all day. The 50 km to Loma Plata on the dirt road seemed so far away. Finally we came to the only hotel in town. Dirty stinky and embarrassed I walked toward a group of young woman. They were talking, no one paid attention to me. I listened to their problems for a while finally I interrupted their conversation. Do you have a room? All were blond, all looked a like. They carried on with their conversation. One got up and helped me at the front desk. We don't have air conditioned rooms available. I don't need it. The nights are cool enough. She gave me a room I took care of Jaco, and showered. Then I joined the group, and just listened to the angry women. These are the modern Mennonites women all belonging to a huge Co-op. Growing crops, raising cattle, processing the milk. They talk about the corruption within the Co-op, injustice and pay and the young men father a young woman, when they are pregnant, they often drop them. They don't want to take responsibility to be a father or get married. They raise the kids alone. That was an eye-opener. I signed the guestbook, she looked at it. She asked me, are you from Canada? No, I said. There are Paul's living around the corner. Are you related to them?? Not that I am aware off.

The Mennonites groups are a state in the state of Paraguay. Their religion doesn't allow the men to serve inmilitary service. To the outside they seem to be a harmonious peaceful worry free religious group, without problems. Boy was I wrong.

It's Sunday morning and I am getting ready to leave, one young man approached me. Is this your bike? Pointing across the courtyard. Yes, I said. You are missing a nut from the rear tire. I couldn't believe it.

We walked over to the bike, he pointed it out. Sure enough. How did that happened? The dirt road does it.

Where can I get one today? Everybody seems to be at church. I got depressed. Here I am on the beginning of my trip and already having problems. He looks over the rest of my bike, it seemed O.K. Where could we get one? Everything is closed. He scratches his head, than he says cheerfully, lets go to the mechanic's home. I followed him on my bike enthusiastic, leaving Jaco at the hotel room. The mechanic seemed to be home. He knocked on the door. A shirtless, disturbed man opened the door. The young man explains my problem. That I am traveling through. He agreed to help wait by my shop. I'll be there in a few minutes. Gladly we waited. He looked at the bike as he went into the shop. I paced worried up and down. It was cloudy, overcast. He showed up with the part. I crossed the fingers hoping it would fit. It didn't fit. Worried, they both went to look again. I stood outside waiting and worring. Smiling then they came to the door. It fit, I was relieved. Thanked them from the bottom of my heart. How much do I owe you? Nothing, I thanked him again For helping me on his day off. We went back to the hotel. I thanked the young man for being so kind. He smiled, its our way of life. Jaco and I set off to Filadelphia 30 kms away. The sand road turned into wet clay. It rained almost all last night, which is unusual for summer. The red clay is sticking to my tires catching between my tire and the fender. The road is slippery. I have great difficulties to keep my bike balanced. The nightmare continues to be a nightmare for the next 500 m The road looks like a fresh plowed field. Thinking to myself I throw my heart ahead of the road and continue driving. I open the throttle sliding bouncing I made it half way through, when my rear tire got stuck in a mud hole. I got off the bike, put it in gear and pushed. The front tire slides in the mud to the side and the rear tire gets deeper. I got angry and frustrated while trying different techniques. No luck. I took a break, looking around I saw a bike coming from a side road. Helpless I waved at him, standing in the mud. He looked unhappy, but gave me a look and stopped. Could you help me? He wasn't thrilled to help. I begged him Finally he parked his bike and came over to get my bike out of the mud. He handed the idling bike to me in the mud, instead of taking it. I asked him politely, could you drive it out of the deep mud? He looked down at me with an attitude. You are the expert I said. I am afraid to get stuck again. Amusingly I watched him sliding through the mud while running behind him. Now taking my bike from him. I said grinning. Thank you big Shot. It wasn't as easy as you thought. I thought he would blow up. The road looked better, but the wet red clay was sticking to my tires blocking the fender. The tire couldn't move a new headache to consider. I looked for a stick to scrape the mud between the fender and the tire. I found one and drove a few meters and the tire was blocked again. I continued to scrape mud out. I remember grandpa telling me, when it rains the clay sticks to your tires and the wheels don't turn. Yes, he was right. The sun came out and it got very hot and blinding me. My head was baking under my helmet so I took it off. Then I realized Jaco was gone. I questioned myself. I panicked and shouted for Jaco. Where are you? No answer. Then I walked around my bike and there he sat in the shade on top of the chain cover. I had to laugh about it. You are the smart one I said. He agreed, I put him on the handlebar to continue driving. Luckily the road improved. It is amazing how fast the sun dried the road. Dirty, frustrated I arrived in Filadelhia to the only hotel in town. It took me two hours for 30 km the road was so bad. The employee knew me from previous visits. I was ready for hearty food. I heard to the north road is closed, due to the rain. Is everything turning against me, I wondered? Or my friends don't want me to go! I looked for the manager to get the latest news. He says, may be later the road will open. These people want the road open, too. Pointing at a group, I joined them, listening to their stories and lies. After they run out of material they turned to me. Where are you going? Driving to America. Everyone's mouth dropped. Alone, they asked curiously? Not really with my parrot I said sarcastically. Boy all a sudden everyone remembered a gangster story. Everyone had advise for me. Internally my hair stood straight. After a while I had enough. Irritated, I said. Why don't you all go to the cemetery and dig a six foot hole and lay there, fill it up and nothing will happen to you. I got up and left. They're trying to run my life, my trip. The manager passed by me could I talk to you? I asked worried, would it be safer to drive thru Argentina than the Chaco? These people scare me! I am driving to the U.S.A. Friendly, he tells me, years ago a family drove with a four wheel truck to Canada through the Chaco. Make sure you have enough water and gas. This is the main problem. It's a desert. I was relieved. On a big map hanging on the wall he shows me the route. A French farm (estancia) and several police stations and military stations. You are fine. A big load fell of my shoulders. I went to see Jaco to share the good news. He was busy terrorizing a young tree. More people came waiting for the road to open. They close wet roads to preserve them. It costs a lot of money to fix and grade them.

America: Final Destination

I met two reporters one from Brazil, one Italian. They took a picture of my bike and me. They promised to send me a picture. I never received it.

I met a young German he was traveling with the American embassy. We become friends and later we shook hands as I told him about my trip. He wished me good luck. The German guy tells me, your bike is not going to make it in the mountains for lack of oxygen. I told him, let that be my worries not yours. You are going with your ambassador to the city. I left him behind. The high society meets in the Chaco, the last frontier. The Mennonites created an oasis in the desert. From time to time I checked, if the road opened

No, I better get a room for the night I tell these reporters. The manager says we are full. Shocked, I say, how about the older rooms without air conditioning? We are completely booked. I should've known that.

You can sleep on the bench outside. I got angry. Well, he continues calmly. We have an old unused building, you can sleep there with your sleeping bag, but don't tell anyone. I promised. He charged me less.

Relieved I took the key. He pointed at the building. The reporters asked, did you get a room? Yes. I said, it's not first class, but a roof over my head, I joked.

Monday morning. The road is still closed. The manager advised me Caesar Chavez is going the same direction. He has a farm (estancia) in Nuevo Asuncion. You can follow him. This gave me security, I was relieved. We sit for hours waiting tensely. Around 11 am the signal came. The road opened. Hurriedly I packed my bike and pulled my protesting parrot Jaco out of the tree. He wasn't happy. No questions allowed. We are leaving. I set him on the handlebar and waved good-bye to everyone. The road was dry and good. We were flying. We came to the first road post and the road was blocked. The guard asked, where are you going? To Mariscal Estagarribia and Mr. Covet is following me. He let me go. The strong sun had dried the road except a few mud holes, but the mud holes got bigger. Now I understood better, why the road is closed. At times I drove on the edge of the road lined with tall grass to avoid the big mud holes. The sun got hotter, so did I. Sweat pouring in a monotone scenery. There in a distance I see something in the middle of the road. Getting my full attention. In a huge mud hole of the wide road, sit's a fire red pickup truck. With two blond boys in the back. They were stuck. I felt sorry for them. While approaching a huge mud hole, which they already passed. I was debating how would I get around it? Just give gas and drive thru. I made it half way and got stuck. It was a deep hole. All techniques didn't help. I have to unload my luggage to get out. The bike stand wouldn't hold up. I couldn't put the luggage in the mud. Jaco climbed on my shoulder scared and looking for shade. Frustrated I shouted for help. No answer. The boys just starred at me. I yell in German for someone to help me. The boys explains,there father went to the house to get the tractor. To pull the truck out. Politely I asked him, could you hold my bike? While I unload it and bring the luggage to the dry side. He understood and didn't mind. We were in the same boat. A very friendly nice boy. Without the luggage the bike got out easily. On the dry road he held my bike, while I loaded. Jaco was sitting on my shoulders supervising. Nothing escaped his eyes. I thanked him several times for his help. My savior. I hoped his dad would come soon. From now on I was very cautious checking every mud hole by foot first.

    My heart was full of joy and happiness. I felt so free at last. There were homes close to the road. People sat in the shade waving at us. I waved back. Not many people are coming through. Jaco was always sitting on the handlebar his wings spread like a happy airplane. Driving for hours in the hot sun and unforgiving heat. The hot wind dries my mouth. I stop from time to time with the motor idling to drink some water. Chewing on limes for quenching thirst. As well as jaco. Every time taking my helmet off, to cool my boiling head.

After hours in the heat. The loneliness I didn't feel like driving. I felt insane. I forced myself to continue. Bushy forest gave way to farmland from flat to rolling hills. The scenery is marvelous. Very impressive. Getting several footbaths, by driving through waterholes. The heat the loneliness, the monotone motor sound got to me! At mini lakes sat ducks, eagles drinking water. What a idyllic scene. I had on my lips to ask excuse me, Mr. eagle, Mr.& Mrs. Duck, how far is it to the border? They looked at us and flew off. The eagle elegantly glided away. I was surprised, happy at the same time. Jaco didn't try to fly with them.

The scenery change from desert to green farmland. Is this the French estancia? Jaco and I enjoyed our drive. I felt so free. Not to worry about paying rent or electric bills.

At one police post he asked me for my bike title. I showed him my buyers contract. I was nervous. I know the police chief from Villaricca. He is my friend, he said smiling. What a surprise. We talked a little and he let me go. Every post asks for I.D. and license. How annoying here in nowhere. I love the country.

It was late afternoon. I heard a steady motor noise. Curiously I slowed down looking over my shoulder. A truck. This must be Mr. Covet. I was excited in a way. Later we drove side by side talking. He didn't know of his luck. That I followed him. The Mennonites suggested that. No problem, he said. Just keep on driving, he said from the passenger side A local Indian is driving him.

We come to a Post. The road is closed. Mr. Covet talks to the officials, they let us through. The sandy road is still wet. The heavy luggage prevents me from driving fast. Having a hard time to keep up. Luckily they stopped for me. Could I put my luggage on the rear, I asked. No problem. He said. From now we were flying. I felt like driving on the beach. Brush on both sides. From time to time I looked over my shoulders to see the truck. Once the truck was gone. My heart fell in my pocket. In shock I thought about my travelers checks in the blue bag. Distrustful I stopped and waited for the truck. Where were you? Checking on a fence. Keep on driving. We are coming. The road got worse. I got stuck a few times. Once the motor wouldn't start. I asked for help. Irritated Mr. Covet gets out. He has trouble getting the motor started. It took a long time. It is very late. Happy but tired, I jumped on the bike and drove off. Dawn came I was still driving. My body felt drained, my nerves had reached its limit. After a while I sat on the side of the road giving up. I was not prepared for that.

    The truck came to my side Mr. Covet asks, what is the matter? I give up I'm exhausted. You can't stay here in the wilderness. It's to dangerous. I wasn't afraid of the wild animals. I am more afraid of the people. He said. At the first post turn right. I listened and continued driving in the dark. I was totally exhausted. Jacob was very calm, patiently sitting on the handlebar. It got cooler and more pleasant, but the drive was endless, forever. Finally on the right appears the post I turned. Mr. Covet passes me, disappears in a white building. I waited. He came out friendly, he says. I talked to the sergeant. You can stay the night. In the morning you can come to our ranch and we'll give you gas. I thanked him.

    A young soldier helped me unloading my luggage and bring it upstairs. A two story building, interestingly, no glass windows. Very basic furniture. Fully dressed I stood in the shower. It felt so good. A pig after a mud bath. I changed into fresh clothes. The sergeant was drunk like a house. I understood it was Sunday night. He invited me for dinner. We sat on the table. Jacob got a chair and we ate silently. I was afraid, unhappy about my hostel. Running footsteps broke the silence. A young soldier ran to the sergeant and whispers something in his ear, while he was eating. Occupied he got up and told me to stay. Both left. Sitting alone I listened. There was a noise I ran to the window. The sky was so dark, I felt I could see all the stars. The country was silent with only a warm breeze blowing. Then I heard the sergeants angry voice, but not the words. I stood like on fire, watching for any movements. In a distance on the ground I saw something white. A swinging belt cut the silence I heard a howl off in the distance Was the the sergeant beating a dog I wondered? I felt anger and sorrow in my heart. The men were walking back to the house. Quickly I sat down on the table, pretending to eat the whole time. I heard footsteps. It was the sergeant and he sat down as if nothing had happened. Curiously I asked what was that noise? A moment of silence. Then he said a young soldier on guard duty fell asleep and someone stole his rifle. This is dangerous. I got mad. Yes, that is terrible to take advantage of him, but you have to understand. It's hard to stand 8 hrs in the sun. Nothing to do. Nobody to talk to. Nothing to read, I was unloading my anger on him. Why aren't there are two of them? Give them shade. He just listened quietly. He didn't respond. After my storm, I asked him. Where do I sleep tonight? The sergeant answers relaxed, with me in my bed! Wrong! Don't you have a spare bed? Seriously he says NO. Alright, realizing I wasn't getting anywhere. I followed him to his bedroom. A queen-size bed with white linen and a mosquito net. Compromising I say to him You have this half of the bed, I have the other half. In the middle is an invisible fence. He didn't care. He just wanted us to lay down. I had no choice. Fully dressed I climbed under the net to my half. No interest in any sex. He was drunk, I didn't trust him. I was stuck for the night with a bunch of men with that brought Goosebumps ran down my spine. I I prayed. Dear lord, help me to make it through the night. The sergeant was sleeping. He hung on me like a monkey, hugging me. I freed myself several times from his arms. I guess he was excited to have a female in his bed. I didn't trusted him, I freed myself from his arm Leave me alone, I said. The breeze coming thru the window felt good. He hugged me again, I gave up, but his excessive body heat made me uncomfortable. I waited until he fell asleep from his overdose of alcohol. Took his heavy arm off my belly, silently I slipped out of the bed. On the bare wood floor was a small mat. My tennis shoes become my pillow. Enjoying the cooler night and hoping the night passes fast. It wasn't comfortable and I felt unsafe. Who knows what he had in mind, when he wakes up. I am out numbered. How did I get into this mess? I wondered. I fell in a light sleep with one eye open. I wake up with the sunrise, afraid to move to wake the sergeant.

He moved touching my side of the bed. I heard him jumping out of bed. Angry footsteps walking around the bed. Suddenly they stopped. I felt him starring at me, as I pretended to sleep. Angry he walked away. Later I got up, checked on Jaco. He sat on his chair, puffed up and his eyes half closed. He looks so funny. I became relaxed. It's morning time to meet the sergeant and release jaco in a tree. It's already hot. We talk about last night. I am not looking for men or sexual adventures. He apologized and I accepted it. I could understand him, being here in this loneliness for so long. He lightened up. We had small talk. We are the same age. Would you let me wash my super dirty bike? He didn't mind, all the younger soldiers were respectful to me. That was a surprise. The bike is clean. I was ready to go. The sergeant begged me to stay and wait for the truck to Bolivia. No, for so long I planned this trip, reading the few available books. Visiting the embassies inquiring for visas. Counting how many countries to pass until America. I am ready to go. I hear the American ambassador saying. You better to take a boat from Peru to America, avoiding central America. Nicaragua. The guerilla war is going on. He heard I was driving a motorcycle. That's why he came to the bullet proof window. I thought he takes the highlight out of my trip. I just nodded. He continued questioning me. I promise to go around central America. I nodded again, looking at the visa. He pushed my passport thru the slot. Relieved I took my passport and ran out of the door.

  For Jaco I had to go to the agriculture office. He advised me, parrots are not allowed to import to USA. Could I get a permit until Mexico? I would be happy with that. He took a long time to write. Again, he reminded me, only until Mexico. While holding the paper. Thank you, let it be my problem. Jaco was sitting on my shoulder the entire time. He agreed with me. I don't leave my pets behind. He goes, where I go. Finally he handed me the paper. Shaking his head he says, what a stubborn girl. All that went thru my head. I turned to the sergeant, I just want to go. You don't have maps. I laughed, what for. There are no road signs in the wilderness. You just follow the sun. The sun tells you the direction. The sun tells you the time. Sometimes you have to read the tire marks at intersections, like the Indians do. He listened quietly. He still preferred I would stay to give him company in the lonelineliness. I understood him well, but I was restless. Saw it as a waste of time to sit around, waiting for a truck. When I have a motorcycle.

  The hot sun was beating on us. Jaco didn't want to leave the tree. You see, your parrot wants you to stay. Listen to him. The distance is calling us, I say firmly as I loaded my bags. Thank you for everything. I waved. The sun had dried the road. Now it was harder to drive in the sand. Jaco was nervous, looking for shade. We drove for an hour. When a house at a corner appeared. This must be the covet's ranch. To be sure I asked the Indian in Spanish. He answered in fluent German. My mouth dropped open. I recovered and drove to the main house. There was a few Indians sitting around. I looked for Mr. Covet as, he leasures from the house with a boy. It was his son, a five year old. I thanked him ironically for last night's cuckoo egg. Calmly he says, you were exhausted. Silence. Curiously I asked. Are all your workers Indian? Yes, they are good honest workers. I teach them German. I was impressed. Admired his gaucho pants. They are cool in the summer, and warm in the winter. His son had come to see jaco. Jaco loves children and their attention. You have a nice ranch here, Mr. Covet. Yes, I enjoy nature and being away from the city. You get gas at the front house. The one you passed.

The Indian man knows the way to Bolivia. He suggests to wait for the truck. The road will become very narrow. The bushes have long needles. The sand is very deep. I got deeply worried. If you come thru again, we'll give you gas again, he says kindly. I thanked him from the bottom of my heart. I do respect the Indians, they live in harmony with nature. I don't think so. I'm going north on my return trip. I'll go thru Venezuela, Guanas, Brazil. I waved and continued driving. There are two police stations until the border. One young soldier stopped me. It was very hot now. I stand in the sun, waiting for the police chief to come. As always I get nervous. When they ask questions. I.D, bike title, where are you going? I said casually to Bolivia. An older man had come, too. Saying to me, wait for the truck. It should come tomorrow. Stubborn I deny. I drive as far as I can. Both men warn me of the deep sandy road. You will get stuck. I continue up the little hill, no tire path to follow. Driving down hill I got off my track and ran into deep sand. Kissing the ground. Knee deep was the sand. It was hard bone work to get the bike up and out of the sand. Jaco had walked away, telling me. It's to hot, I'll be waiting in the shade. I had no choice, struggling to get out of the sand, unloading all the bags. I parked on solid ground. Reloaded, soaked in sweat and in my boots. I took a deep breath and called for jaco. Luckily. He answered, but where is he? A green bird in a tree! I continued calling. Jaco, where are you? He answered, hello, hello. I looked and looked while the sun fried my head, I got frustrated and annoyed. He must be here. I hear him. Finally I located him on a thorny, thick branched tree. He sat comfortably in the shade, a wild breeze blowing. While I sweat bullets in the unforgiving sun. Jaco had no interest to leave the tree and was fighting me. I talked calmly to him, finally he let go of the branch. I put him on the handlebar. Happy, I continue, but the motor wouldn't start. I tried many times, nothing helped. Jaco started pacing up and down the handlebar. I have no choice than to return to the police station. It is a very hard to push the bike uphill in the deep sand. I was swearing and sweat pouring down my body into my boots with long pants. Jaco searched for shade. I talked to him calmly, be patient. We are almost on the top of the hill. There I sat on the bike, rolling down the hill surprising the soldier. They didn't hear me coming. I told them of my accident and the motor wouldn't start. Could you get the boss? One soldier went to get him. He was surprised to see me so soon. I told him about the incident. In the background by the barracks I saw a woman with two children. I was relieved. I asked if I could stay, apologizing for my stubbornness. He agreed a little grumpy, but he agreed. They showed me a room on the second floor. Very nice with a clean shower. I felt in heaven. I unloaded the bike checked on my German chocolate in the mini cooler. All the ice had melted. I gave the chocolate to the soldier to throw them away.

  Police chief Chaves and his family are very nice. They live at the end of the second floor corridor. They live in nature with goats, cows, horses and birds. It felt good to rest. In the evening at dinner I learned that actually several families live on the station, in little homes. One cook is cooking for all officers and their families. The next day the truck didn't come. I worked on my bike to get the engine started. I checked the water level on my battery. The days passes. No truck. It felt good to rest, I didn't realize how tired my body was from packing, running around in Villarica - Asuncion. Jaco was content to be in a tree every day. At night he sleeps in my room. It's nice here. On my forced vacation, but hope the truck is coming soon.

One day I heard crackling on the ground I pick up little papers. The chocolate papers. They must have eaten and licked the papers. I smiled to myself. They had some goodies in this loneliness. A light came on, that's why they are so friendly. At 3 am, I hear a whistle, voices. Is it the truck? I think the police chief went outside and returned after a while. False alarm. I went back to sleep. I waited until the morning to ask the old man Acuna Who was that? He explained to me Every time somebody comes thru the chief has to get up, check their papers. There are whisky smugglers traveling the two unofficial borders. I thought, how exciting. A real adventure. When is the truck coming, was on everyone's mind. I learned the bell ringing is for changing the guards. The soldiers cook their own food. Everyday is a different soldier cooking. I never saw them in our mess hall, but one cook for the families and us. Every afternoon the three families play volleyball. On the beginning I played, but found it boring. Approximately 35 people live here. It was vacation on a farm. Working for what? When you can live without it. In the evening the groups gather and drink whiskey, talk, look at the stars. One day a man came on horse from Garray. The last military station before the border. Then they brought a big road grader for export. That was the excitement of the day.

The soldier work the fields, cut the grass around the houses to keep snakes away. The wild Emus and chickens eat the bugs. I lollygagged all day. I was surprised how many tourists are coming thru on tour buses.

The third day I explored the grounds, and big cactus with red fruits. An infinite desert so far the eye can see. I visited the cook in the kitchen. In the afternoon the captain from Garay came to visit. Later I learn he is called a woman hunter. I feel safe here. No truck.

The fourth day. A horse rider comes from the estancia Caesar Covet in traditional gaucho pants to buy whisky. I took a picture of him. Learn. Caesar Covet served his military duty here and ended up staying. He started a ranch - estancia. He named it Nuevo Asuncion. His father works for the government and owns several factories in Asuncion. How interesting and exciting to live on this famous police station in the Chaco. Everybody knows everyone. I did daily my fill-in puzzles, which my father bought me. Acuna helped me. He is an intelligent man. He lived in Argentina and owned a farm then with a broad vision. I enjoyed talking to him and listing to his stories. When we were alone. He harassed me, to sleep with him. Disgusted and in rude voice I asked him. Isn't there anything else on your mind than sex, women or trucks? We are all nervous, wondering when the truck is coming.

I did my puzzles to pass the time and stay calm, doing something. The truck will come. I say calmly. Jaco sat daily in the tree. Three trucks are coming from Bolivia, we all got excited. The police chief informed us. They were not returning. The road is bad. They had to drive slow, a nerve breaking trip. Sad, disappointed I went to my room. Thinking of my friends. They are probably wondering, where I am. Mentally I was ready for the trip. Jaco called me. Mama, mama, his way of saying I am hungry. Stopped my thoughts and went to feed him.

Fifth day. Thunder and lightening announces a storm. Strong winds blow bending the trees, and raining hard this morning. Our hope for the truck coming soon is foolish. We are stuck. Sixth day. No truck, our patience is wearing thin. The wait drives us up the wall. It's February 9th and I am still in the Chaco! Today is our cooks 36th birthday, with food supply low. There was no cake. We celebrated at night relaxing under the star filled sky sipping whiskey. The seventh day, over breakfast sipping hot yerba tea, I said the truck has to come. One from Asuncion to restock the food supply. The other from Bolivia. The patience from the four of us is at the end. Later we played cards, games and my puzzle day in day out. At night we sit under the moon light to save energy, while drinking our whisky. To calm our nervous. Eight day. That night I dreamt a truck came with two wild looking men. Every morning I get up, leave my room to the balcony over seeing the road. There was a parked truck. I pinched myself to believe it, so it wasn't a dream. I jump from joy, with excitement. We are leaving. I ran downstairs to see the men. They looked tired, somewhat scary. Like half monkey, left over's from the stone age. Acuna shows up, the men talk. When are we leaving I finally ask the men. Their looks give me Goosebumps. The weather has been bad, lots of rain. Two days ago, they decided to leave. The machines are needed. Later on, we load. Some machine parts and my bike. I was happy. Then one Bolivian, Gonzalez tells me. Usually we continue to Filadelphia to have parties. Drink whisky and have sex with western girls. Firm, determined I looked him in the eyes, I better drive my bike. I was scared, but not showing it. He warned me. The road is very bad, deep sand, the thorn bushes will rip your clothes off. At intersections you don't know what road to take. You are safer driving with us. I had mixed feelings and mistrust. I felt trapped. These men were in no hurry. They took their time for everything.

America: Final Destination

After lunch we left. I thanked the police chief several times, for his hospitality. Acuna sat in the driver cabin, I sat with the other men in back of the truck in the shade. It was another hot day. A breeze made it more pleasant. Passing thorny bushes and cactus. This wilderness is survival of the fittest. After a 40 minute drive we arrive in Garay at 2pm. It took an hour to get my passport stamped. The captain thin like a rail, asks many questions. He is known as a woman hunter. I was forewarned. I told him several times, I am not looking for men, he finally gave up. Stamped my passport. It was a tense situation. Now we are officially leaving Paraguay, I thought. Looked for the truck, parked off the side under a tree. A couple of men sit with others leaning against a big bottle tree. I join them waiting. Overlooking a huge junk yard with lots of old machines. This is suppose to be a military station? Why does he collects all that? I asked Gonzalez's brother. This all goes to Bolivia. I was shocked. Hours passes. What are we waiting for? And whom? I asked. I wanted to go. The Bolivians were laid back, chewing cocoa leaves with baking soda, it forms a ball and takes the hunger and sleep away. We have no diesel, he mumbled. I knew I have to control my patience, my restlessness and lay back, too.

    Suddenly two midsize camping buses with tourists arrive. They stop, everybody runs to the bathrooms. Curious, I ask, where are they coming from? Their safari tour starts in Ecuador, and they come from different countries. The horny captain shows up with his camera, jumping around to take pictures of the girls in bikinis. Some posed for him. I had to laugh about him. This was hilarious. The bus driver hurried them on the bus. I was excited for the tourists even for my own trip, ahead. It gave me Goosebumps. My middle name is travel. I wished them a good trip in my poor English. At 7 pm we leave, the road barrier closes behind us. I lived here one year and seven months. It felt like a lifetime. I waved. Good-bye Paraguay. We are finally driving, I'm so excited, full of joy. We enter a dark forest with long needles, scratching on both sides of the truck. The sandy road got deeper and narrower. This goes on for hours, just the monotone sound of the motor. Supposedly jaguars live here, I didn't see one though. It's getting cooler and fresher. I bundled up, hoping and prayed we would make it safe to Bolivia with these men. And I won't spend 10 days with Acuna in Camiri. I want to go on my way to America. As soon as the sun went down, it got really cold. I was surprised at how chilly it was. Acuna invited me to join the warm cabin. I refused, I preferred to stay with jaco and my bags. Later they put a heavy canvas tarp over us for the cold, but we couldn't see, which made the trip more boring. I made a hole on the side to see. We passed thru a few intersection, it was very cold. I was actually glad not to be driving, I wouldn't know what road to take. The truck stopped. Acuna and the driver walk away to talk to a soldier, for a long time. I peek out of my hole. What are they discussing? Maybe or probably controlling the smugglers, they want a piece of the pie. We continue in the middle of the forest. A shelter made from branches, very primitive, but well built with a bed. Like forgotten from the last war. The road gets worse, along with huge waterholes. At times the truck stops, he walks the road first, to check how to drive it. Late at night, we stop at a clearing. The full moon gives us light. Why do we stop, I asked being intrusive. We got to eat. Under the motor hood he brings a big cloth covered cheese out. That's funny. I bring bread sticks. We eat, relax, enjoy looking at the moon. The rough road continues, sleep is far from my mind. To cold and bumpy. Fearing to get stuck again goes through my mind. The road grader stops ahead of us. The driver talks to Acuna. He has a problem, Acuna stays with him to get it fixed in the morning. A farmer close by comes, offers to help. They can stay with him the night. Acuna turns to me concerned, wait for me in Camiri. I said,may be! Again he offers the warm cabin to me. Now I get inside. Acuna begged me to wait for him. I just nodded. The warm felt good. I asked Gonzalez what is the problem with the machine. They lost a tire. I was relieved to get rid of Acuna. We talk a little. Later I ask how is the way to Sucre? He looked surprised, why do you want to go there? It's a historical city, a scenic road, I say excited. He shakes his head, the road is very bad. You are better off going to Sta. Cruz, Cochabamba most of the road is asphalt. It turned out Acuna is his best friends. They work hand in hand. He buys in Asuncion and brings the machines to the Chaco, from there they import them to Bolivia. My feeling is, he is dumb as a fox and knows more than he admits. My main concern was to get safe to Camiri, get my bike fixed, and hit the road north.

Vivian, Renate, and my mom on a boat trip in Rio, Brazil

My parrot, Jaco. A true friend

My good friends, Roswitha and her husband, Julian Escobar in Villarrica, Paraguay

Roswitha and Julian at their home in Villarrica

My good friends, Ramona and Reinaldo Alderete in Villaricca, Paraguay

Their daughter, Maria Mercedes, and her husband Walter. He is a doctor in the German colony

Grandpa Schade and his wife at their daughter, Elisa, and Willy's wedding

Mr. Metzgers and his son and two daughters in the colony Independencia

Bolivian truck at the police station "Nueva Asuncion" with some staff. February, 1987

Leaving Paraguay in 1987
Border control
"Garray" in Chaco

BOLIVIA

At 3 am we arrive in Boyiulbe. A military station in the desert. The official Bolivian border. They open at 6 am I heard, till then I tried to sleep, but it was to cold. Gonzalez offered to warm me. No, thank you. At 6 am, we learn we have to wait until the major arrives. We were all bumped out, searching for a warm spot in the rising sun in this lovely place. It seemed the time stood still here. At 8 am the doors open. The sergeant invites me into a Adobe building, asking for my passport. He takes it and walks away. The room is very cold as a tomb, I was freezing. After a while he returns, says we are going to do a through investigation of the truck. We all see red. He finds a revolver, a sleeping bag. He turns to Gonzalez. You shouldn't have a military sleeping bag. Angered, upset we stood by, listening to the terrorizing sergeant. He critizes everything. I jump in the conversation, defending my companions. Gonzalez got called to see the major in the office. We sat on the back of the truck soaking in the warm sun. my frozen bones appreciated it. After a long wait, the three appeared chatting. Nobody was in a hurry, but I wanted to go. The major turns to me, asking questions, the sergeants takes over, requesting my bike title. I refused to show it to him, while digging in my bags. I feel, he is holding us up from traveling. I have only a sales contract, most vehicles in Paraguay are stolen from Brazil, including mine. He argues with me about the German laws. My mouth drops open, how does he know that? In the middle of nowhere in Bolivia? I think this sergeant should have a sign around his neck: beware of dog. He continues bickering with me. Suddenly the major turns to me with a big smile, asks friendly. Do you have the bike papers? Surprised and firm I say. Yes, sir. I went to get it. The major interrupts me, says smiling. I don't need to see them, so long you have them. Where are you going? To America, I said relieved. He handed me my passport. I thanked him with a big smile. He wished me a good trip in German. Turned to the Bolivians. You can go now. Hurriedly we leave, taking one last look at the angry sergeant. If I would light a match, he would explode. My joy was short lived. We stop for customs. I was horrified. Gonzalez looks at me and laughs. These are my friends. I was not convinced. In a few days they'll give me my revolver back. He walked away. We hung around and waited. I was nervous not understanding their behavior. I paise up and down on the gravel road, lined with gray dusted bushes to pass the time. A young boy with a cloth covered basket approached me, offering empanadas. I have no Bolivian money, I tell him. Out of nowhere came Gonzalez, grabbed a empanada and handed it to me. Try it, he says motivating. I take a bite, it tastes good. Filled with veggies, not meat like in Paraguay. Gonzalez nods, satisfied and walks away. The Paraguayan joins me wondering. Why we hang around for so long? It's his first trip, too. We watch the men, disappearing in a long adobe building. We wonder, what will be next?

Several men appear talking, laughing. They ask me to come to the office. I have an uneasy feeling. The officer tells me seriously. You can't leave the Sta Cruz County, because you have no transit papers. They would take your bike. Angry I reply, what transit papers? Quietly concerned he looks at me, thinking. Then he smiles, Gonzalez can get you one. He is a good guy. I was not convinced. I would prefer you give me one. He smiles again, get it from Gonzalez. He is my friend. Realizing I had no other choice.

Later I questioned and terrorized him for this transit paper. Why can't I leave the county? No answer. Frustrated I think has my trip already ended? Thinking of my friends in Paraguay. I brooded over an escape plan, somehow I will make it. The scenery is getting very nice, mountains, farmland, the bushes lining the road are covered with red dust. We stop almost in every town. He drives me mad. I am tempted to unload my bike and drive.

We are passing thru many rivers, I found it very exciting. Around noon, it was very hot, sticky we arrive in a bigger town, many people wave at him, he waves back. The circus is coming to town, I think to myself. We stop at a modest hotel. He tells me to wait. As soon as he was gone, I climbed on the back of the truck, getting my luggage ready. After a long wait, he returns. I think, that wash woman talks forever. Friendly, he says, this is your hotel. We unload my luggage, jaco in his cage. The next thing is my bike. No, he says. We unload that later. Why, I protested. He refused. Skeptical I chained my bike to a heavy machine part. Very unhappy I asked him. When will you bring my bike? After lunch, he said grumpy. They left. I registered at the hotel. She gave me a nice room with a shower. A good bed my back appreciated it. After lunch I went to the reception. Everyone is friendly. The girl knew some English. Do you have Gonzalez's phone number? She did, I called him. When do I get my bike and I want it now and I don't like you driving it. He promised to come shortly. Impatiently I waited in the street. I spotted the Paraguayan coming on foot, almost hysterically I ask, where is my bike? Calmly he says. I need the key, you chained the bike to the truck. I forgot it. Could I come with you? No, he says firm, because of his wife. I handed him the key for the chain. Surprised he takes it, and the bike key? No, I come along or you push it. Again, I waited and waited. Afraid to loose my bike. There I saw the Paraguayan pushing my bike to the hotel. Relieved I run to him and thanked him several times. After he left I asked the receptionist, do you know a mechanic? She smiled, yes, I do. Could you call him? I hardly understand their dialect. She did, we stood around waiting. He will be on foot. He just sold his motorcycle. A young man with Indian features, black hair shoulder length appeared. I stared at him for a minute. That's him I asked speechless. Not what I expected. She greets him, they talk. Then he turns to me, introduces himself. Excited I explain my problem, hoping to get it fixed. He wanted to see the bike, the girl guided him, while talking consistently to him. I waited by the entrance watching them. They came back, she tells me, Willy wants to take the bike to his shop. Could I come along? I have nothing to do. He didn't mind, I handed him the key. I was very protective of my bike, my only transportation. He pulls into his driveway, two Doberman dogs behind a gate greets us. I started to like Willy. He put the dogs away, his grandmother greets us. He drives the bike to the back yard, his work area. Motorcycle parts lying around everywhere. A few papaya trees provide shade. Smiling he says, that is my place. I think a typical mechanic and good looking. He brings me a chair to sit. It's hot, humid, sticky, unpleasant in long pants and boots. He talks I hardly understand him. He inspects the bike and takes the air filter out. It was super dirty. That is your only problem. I was so happy, he diagnosed the problem. He worked very slow, laid back, asking many questions. Two little kids showed up. Curious I ask, are these your kids? No, my sisters. I am not married, he answers laughing. That is a surprise. What is your sister doing? She bakes custom cakes. She has three kids, no husband. Later his sister shows up to get her kids. Surprisingly she is white with black hair. He is dark skinned, black hair. It makes nice kids. Coffee with milk, we both laugh. The message was that could be us. I felt my face flush, I hoped my face didn't turn red. Think, here I am on my way to America and I run into a man! I had given up on men. Why didn't I met him earlier? The world is upside down. Willy asks, what do you do? Bake cakes. Now his sister Lenny asks me. If I would like to see her cake album? Sure, I would like to. The cakes are outstanding, impressive, great decoration, different to Germans. You like sweets? I ask willy. No, he says. I could understand. In generally they are very sweet, here. When I needed to use the bathroom we passed his grandmothers parrot. He looks like mine. Willy shares his dislike for the parrot. He screams every afternoon. Yes, I have one just like it at the hotel. I like to ring his neck, he continues. I love parrots and went to the bathroom. After he finished the bike, I ask him. Could you show me the city tomorrow? He agreed. How much do I owe you? He shook his head, nothing. It was only a dirty air filter, but it took him hours. I was surprised and flattered.

Jaco woke me early the next morning with his beak and he rattled the carrier door. Saying let me out! I went to ask the receptionist, if Jaco could sit in the vines? Sure, she said friendly. He spends all day there. Whistling, the female turned around and sees nobody. I laugh about him. His favorite game. Willy comes Bolivian time, late. I am just glad he shows up. I was excited for the tour. He shows me every corner of the town and surroundings, I couldn't get a better tour guide. We visit the old bridge, the small airport, a mountain top with several cruses. The sewage water treatment plant, the cementary and his fathers grave. He is an excellent driver and everyone seems to know him many people wave at us. At times I wanted to hug him, but how would he react? So I didn't. At noon we return. He has to work. I go to my hotel room, I have seen a lot this morning and need to digest everything. People are so friendly. What should I do? Stay or continue? These transit papers haunt me. I think of my Paraguayan friends. They would be disappointed if I would stay. I am on a mission to write a book about my trip and learn more Taek-won-do techniques. I will resist all temptations. Don't start what you can't finish. Take the risk to loose willy's friendship. I tell him in a diplomatic way. I don't want to hurt his feelings. I went to see Gonzalez for my papers. He wasn't home. A German man told me about his pitfalls in Bolivia. I think it is not the country's fault, he lost everything. I've seen and heard many similar stories. They trust the wrong people, they put all their eggs in one basket and loose everything. They have no money to return to Germany. They become drunks, and nuisances. He warns me the road through the mountains is bad. It's not a freeway like in Germany. That's why I am here. I will fight the battle. He looks at me and I get up. I will tell Gonzalez you were here. On the way to the hotel a bike driver stops me. He is from the hotel warning me of Gonzalez. I was trusting him now I telling him the transit paper story. He thinks it's all baloney, he is trying to steal your bike. I thanked him for the insight. It left me an emotional roller coaster. Stewed for hours. I needed to talk to someone. In the afternoon I went back to Willy. He was surprised to see me. He stopped working and invited me to meet his entire family for tea. It was hard to express my feelings. Why should I go to Sta. Cruz? He suggests go through the mountains just like I had planned. He wrote a list of towns to pass. I was relieved later he accompanied me to the hotel. I told him I'll see Gonzalez tonight one last trial to get these transit papers. He doesn't like him. Later I ran into Gonzalez and it became a warm evening. I confront him about the papers. He laughs, lets have a beer and dinner. It was the same restaurant I had lunch. He ordered beers. He voided answering my questions, and I got more angry and was ready to go. A couple of men next to our table butted in our conversation. Did you bring chickens from Paraguay? One asks. No, she is a tourist, says Gonzalez for me. About that time an angry woman with a child in tow. She appeared at the window yelling at Gonzalez, waving her umbrella. I better go. Fast he says, stay, it's alright. Three men from the next table started talking to us, one was from France. I felt terrible. I don't want to be you tonight, I tell Gonzalez in private. He just laughed. We got involved in conversations and drank lots of beer.

Saturday morning I awoke with a hangover. I went one more time to Willy's to say, good-bye. And share the depressed news. He sent me to the transit department. I went on foot. He listened to me and his harsh answer is, I radio to the stations, that you will be traveling. I was somewhat relieved. It was a boring Saturday afternoon, what should I do? I returned to willy to pass the news. He was skeptical, didn't you asked for the papers? Yes, he refused, but he will radio it in. I spent the afternoon with him and his family. They wanted me to stay. I can't. I promised to return after one year. My friends in Paraguay are waiting for me. He doubted my word. We exchanged addresses. Early Sunday morning I pack my bike. It was fresh, I sat Jaco on the handlebar, with a sparkle in his eyes he spreads his wings. I was rather depressed, I couldn't sleep well last night. A cool brise blowing wakes me up. We drive through the quiet, empty streets. I felt like a thief, stealing myself out of town. The cornerstones turned into dirt road. The first road barrier. I stop to go inside to pay the road toll. A man sits on a table, eating his breakfast. I hand him the fee. You don't have to pay, but paid him anyway to avoid trouble. Passing peaceful farmland, grazing horses and cows. It's fresh and I am driving I didn't notice a flock of parrots were flying over my head. Then they screamed. Jaco answered their call and flies after them. My heart almost stops. I thought his wings were clipped, but he was flying. I drive behind him as fast as I could, but then he flew off the road to the right into a branchy tree. I called Jaco, but he doesn't answer. I called repeatedly. Frustrated I stood on the road, trying to locate Jaco in the tree, which was 100 yards away. Very tall sea grass separates us. Then a tall wooden fence sits behind is the tree. Is it marsh or wetlands? Will I sink in by walking through? All sort of thoughts went through my head. I call Jaco again, finally he answered. I was relieved to know he is there. What should I do? Scratching my head, should I let Jaco be free? Free with his own kind? I get determined to have him out of the tree. I look left and right. There comes a man and a boy walking, I waited on them. They came close. Is it safe to walk thru the grass? He looks confused. Now I explain, why I'm depressed and what happened. He volunteered to get Jaco. Are you sure? I ask, surprised. He said something to the boy and walked into the grass. We couldn't see him, only the tops of the grass moved. Then he climbed the fence to the tree. I can't see a parrot, he yells back. I called Jaco, he came to the lower branch visible for us on the road. So we yelled back and forth for directions. It was a long, mentally exhausting deal. One moment he sees Jaco, then he goes away. I was tempted to come to help, but he needed the help from the street. I tell Jaco to get on the stick. We watch him climb down the fence, disappearing in the tall grass. My heart was pounding soaked in sweat from the excitement, waiting to see them. Here they come. We were so happy to get reunited. I thanked the man several times for his help. Now I tie a rope on Jaco's foot to prevent him from flying away. He hated it. At every opportunity he got he tried to get it off. He was unbalanced. I wrapped a T-shirt on the handlebar to give him a better grip on this rough road. He protested the rope. Sorry I don't take anymore chances. I need you! I don't want to drive alone. We are friends. We enter the humid rainforest, it is lovely. We see many birds flying, chirping. Many black birds with some yellow and blue. It is a wonderful world. Luckily Jaco is minding his business. He as well enjoys the chirping, the songs from the birds while steadily driving up the mountains. A creek follows the road. The water is crystal clear. A very romantic drive. A small steep hill and a huge rock on the right awakes me of day dreaming. In shock I stop. I shift in first gear, open the throttle, but the heavy luggage pulls me down. Then I try to make it up the rock. The front tire losses its grip, the luggage pulls the bike down. We crash in the deep sand. The gas is leaking. Jaco runs nervous up and down on the handlebars. Frustrated, swearing I fight to get the bike upright. It was easier said then done. The back tire kept on sliding away. I cursed like a champion. At least the gas stopped leaking. I was holding the bike off the ground. After many efforts, the bike stood. I take a deep breath, and talk calmly to Jaco. My good companion now he relaxes, too. We take a short break while I catch my breath. The breeze dries my soaked body. Ready to start the engine. No reaction, I try again and again. Nothing, I get worried. Is the sparkplug all the way in? Does the battery has enough water? Everything looks OK, but the engine won't start. I throw my arms in the air. What can I do? Here alone in this wilderness? Wait? It could be days before someone comes. I hear the man's prediction, you won't make it. That motivated me and said loud calmly. Yes, I will make it. I will show them. How wrong they are. I let the engine cool off. Enjoy the silence interrupted only from the bird squeaks. It is wonderful here, my eyes are wondering. Looking up into the trees. A green sky with sunrays shinning through. It was so peaceful. looking down to the creek, up and down the road day dreaming. Then a genius light comes on. I unload the bike and pushed the bike of the road and on the hillside. Everything else has failed so far. I pull the choke to let more air in the engine and it started right away. My heart jumped of joy, as well Jaco's. We let the engine warm up, while unloading the luggage and walking up the hill. Then comes the moment, I guide the bike up the goat trail, while I walk on the steep hill. One wrong step and I end up in the creek down below. I sweat from excitement and fear, the bike is quit heavy. Just focus and look straight ahead I tell myself. We made it, Jaco. Cheering to him. This was quit an experience. I found solid ground to park and load the luggage. We continue our trip, steadily uphill. It was a very windy road, I was able to drive only in second gear for hours like a snake. Hoping and talking to the engine not to give up. The forest stays behind me. We take a break with the engine idling, not taking any chances. I take my helmet off a fresh breeze dries my sweaty hair. I took a picture. Admiring the breathtaking view. The forest covered mountains, green valleys, no towns, no people just us and nature. That's the way I like it. On the top we even get a better panoramic view. Huge green canyons and a valley just like the grand canyons in Arizona, USA. I debated to take pictures with my camera. They wouldn't come out well. My eyes take better pictures. Again enjoying the silence and peace. A fresh breeze blows, I was soaked in sweat which gave me a chill. Why? It's hard work driving these roads, I joked to Jacob lets continue. He always looks happy. On these breaks Jaco takes the opportunity to chew on my break cables. He thinks the plastic is for him. I had to disappoint him, by wrapping a T-shirt around it. I look ahead the road is going down, what a nightmare, but I have to continue encouraging myself. I stay on the mountainside and don't look down and drive slowly. I have one eye on the road, the other on the beautiful scenery. On the way we cross many rivers, a real adventure. A first time experience for me. When a big wide river came in sight, I stop first, making sure the luggage is tight. Are you ready, Jaco? In low gear we enter the river not knowing how deep the water will be. Goosebumps run down my spine from excitement.

The water was not as deep as I expected. Except a couple of times it reached the engine. Jaco are you having fun? He did a little dance in confusion. Jaco this is real adventure, real fun. I got my bike and boots washed at the same time. It was a wide long river drive, luckily no water entered the engine, I was holding my breath. Later on along the road stood a house and several trucks parked along the roadside. I stop, kids come running, shouting loud, un loro (a parrot). Jaco enjoys the commotion, he talks and whistles. A man joins us, to see what's going on. I ask my question, he answers, but first come to have lunch with us. Is it already lunch I ask surprised. Yes, it's 1 pm. Behind the house is a long table, a group of people sit, talk and eat at the same time. They give me a plate of food to join in. Jaco gets corn on the cob, which he adores. Eating happily and still talking. The Bolivians talk about the road condition and the distance to Sucre. I learned it took me 6 hours to drive 145 km, wow. Three big trucks carrying charcoal. They offer me to drive with them. They predict the road gets worse ahead. Thank you for the offer, I keep on driving, slowly but surely. I sensed they would love to have my company, however I was cured from the last ride. Everybody said" provecho" thank you for the meal, gets up and leaves. I ask the owner. How much do I owe you for the meal? Nothing. I needed gas, he charged me triple for that. I continue the drive. Once again I got stuck in mud puddles. It took me a long time to get out. Jaco was nervous. He doesn't like the stops, I wished he could help me physically, that would really help. Jaco calm down, we are getting out. He listened and looked at me. The road gets more challenging, I force myself to continue driving. Two girls hang on a fence, I stop they ask curiously, where are you going? I tell them. They smile, say. "you are so macho." They surprise me. I feel encouraged and continue my trip in the mountain. They live in a small adobe houses, small low doors, you have to bend to get inside. They seem so happy, here in the country. Later on going uphill I see a frightful man sitting on the edge of the road looking downhill. I wondered what is he doing here alone in nowhere? I wasn't about to stop and pass him up distrustful. I look down the mountain and see a bus laying on its side. The roof was loaded with luggage. I hope he doesn't get a wrong parking ticket. I hoped for the man someone will help him. I was glad not to be driving in a bus. In a small town Monte Guido, I stop to ask for directions. The truck driver gives me directions and tells me to wait at the end of the town at the road service station. I do. The roadbarriar is closed. So I wait. The truck arrives shortly after. The older man tells me now, the road ahead is very bad. They had a lot of rain. We'll load your bike in the back. I trusted him. He knew best. He has that karma. I sit with the two men in the driver cabin. The dumb truck with high wheels had problems to get through these waterholes. The old man like a father to the young driver gives him instruction on where to pass and how to handle the road. We never got stuck. We talked very little just starring at the road. The older one turns to me, sitting in the middle, you would not have made it. I admitted I've would had, had a very difficult time on my own. It takes us three hours to get to Rio Acero. We see many farmers, they plant mostly yucca, corn, peanuts, potatoes and chili peppers. We pass through the national park. The poor farmers burned more forest to get more farmland. Which is prohibited, but they do it anyway. The last rain caused a huge mudslide from the mountains. They plant a lot on the hills. People, animals are wading through the mud searching for their few belongings. I didn't see Red Cross or any other outside help. It was painful to see and watch these sad faces. Nothing we could do. The old man says calmly, they help themselves and each other. I can't forget that sight. It looked like pigs taking a mud bath with concerned faces. Rio

America: Final Destination

Acero has may be 10 homes along the road going uphill on the left. On the right is the road service station. It is a cloudy, humid afternoon. We unload my bike and luggage. On foot I go to find a bed for the night. The locals frowned and showed their dislike for foreigners. There was no free bed anywhere. They scoffed at me, go away. It started to get colder. Frustrated I returned to the station. Do you have a spare bed or a dry corner to crash for the night? The young man looks terrified. No, these are only men dormitories. I protested, I can't sleep in the wet cold street. What I am suppose to do? Supposedly there is no free bed anywhere! He went to talk to the boss while I waited in the street. He returns and says you can have my bed, I'll sleep in the truck. No, let me sleep in the truck, you have your bed. He insisted to take his bed. So he shows me to the room with three beds. A candle on the window seal. How romantic I think. The bed in the corner will be yours tonight. Calmly he continues, the boss talked to the men. No one will bother you. I was relived to have a place to sleep. Jaco stayed in the warm kitchen. The men come in and we chat for a while before going to bed. Everyone is respectful and friendly. Fully clothed I snuggle under three blankets to stay warm. It rained all night. That's bad news. I get disappointed for the set back s of my trip. I looked forward so long. I went to see the boss, he advised me to wait. He radios the other road stations. They all confirm the road is bad and closed. I thanked him for his help and letting me stay the night. Into our conversation, he says, he has a teenage daughter. If she would be traveling, he would be glad somebody would help her. I was deeply touched from his honesty and felt for the the people. I went to visit Jaco in the kitchen. He had fun with the young kid and testing all the ingredients she had. She goes to bake bread in a brick oven outside. It is a cloudy day, a little chilly. The young man and I walk down to the bridge visiting a nearby house. All eyes are on us.

Surprised! Today everybody is friendly to us. A man is carving a wooden bowl, proudly he shows it off. A rain day is a holiday. No one works in the field. They stay home. We walked back. One woman brings her young child outside to let it urinate in the street. They have no toilets. I was shocked. Women wear mostly their national wool woven skirts. One sits at the door on the ground, we look over her shoulder. She is knitting a colorful scarf, it's beautiful I commented. She smiles. We visit with more farmers, some ask me surprised. Are you travel alone? You are so macho! The first night I heard howling. What is that I ask curiously the men in my room. The locals communication! Wow! The young man let me have his bed another night. I was embarrassed. In the early morning I felt something. I open my eyes and see a hand moving into the bed, getting closer to me, I hold his hand, whisper looking for something? The young man sleeping on the floor with a blanket whispers, I like to get into my bed. The truck is very cold. You can have your bed and I sleep on the floor. No, he denies quickly.

It's Tuesday morning, still cloudy, but it didn't rain last night. What a relief. I was ready to go, I thanked everybody for their hospitality and the bed. I put Jaco on the handlebar, off we drove. Morning mist is hanging over the rainforest and mountains. A beautiful sight, breathtaking views I am so excited to see this.

Several times I moved fallen branches, moved fallen trees blocking the road and passing through many mud holes. This is not the German highway, but the beautiful scenery makes up for it. It started to drizzle than turned into a cold rain. I stop to put my raincoat on. My hands and feet are stiff and frozen. Jaco enjoyed the rain from time to time he shook the rain off his feathers. He looked happy. He didn't want a rain cover. I am so happy to have him. People standing in their doors of their homes

America: Final Destination

sticking their head out to see who is crazy enough to drive in that rain. I smile at them, sometimes I wave. While keep on driving trying to escape the rain. The rainforest gives way to agriculture and pasture. It is amazing to see such variety. One said, pure vegetables. The locals eat a lot of veggies. In Paraguay they eat mostly meat and yucca. Little veggies are to much work to grow. I come to Rosal and see a gated Oil refinery. At a little stand stands a man starring at me. It's over cast, a little drizzling. I approach him, ask politely. Could you sell me gas? He asks for my passport. I hand it to him. He verifies it and gives me direction to go in the back. I see a pump, but not a single soul. Confused I look around. Waiting in the cold. Finally two men come. I was cold and shivering inside. I ask them, could I get gas now? He fills my tank. You need oil? No thank you, I said confused. They continue asking me questions. Exhausted I ask after a while. Is this a police station? No, they say friendly. How much do I owe you? Nothing. I was stunned that's unusual. The boss handed me my passport and wished me a good trip. Happy and relieved I thanked him. I drove away, thinking what a strange situation. Strange people I can't figure them out. Continuing through the mountain comes the town of Tacobucco with a traditional cloth factory. I enjoy their original colorful clothing. I drive through downtown while looking around. Suddenly the road was gone, I looked down the hill and see the remains of the road. The rain washed it away. Once again I didn't see a Red Cross or other charities helping. Passing people looked at me and point in a direction. I understood that's the detour. No smiling faces, all are serious. Many chewing coca leaves to curb hunger and the altitude 2000m high. Eucalyptus trees line the street before entering or leaving a town. Since the Indians walk long distances they can rest in the shade. Welcome, I think in humor. In these small towns the time stands still. They stick to their old tradition. I really enjoyed that. A woman is herding goats and cows with big huffs. Under her arm she carries wool, while walking she is spinning the wool around to a stick. No time is wasted, they have a rough life and the Indians amaze me. From the 50 kilogram nylon bags they make fishnets. Donkeys are used to carry heavy loads. They treat them well and feed them well. They are not stubborn like people say.

I stop in Zudanec at the open air market. The kids come running and shouting. Un loro, un loro (a parrot). Everybody wants to touch him, I warn them. Jaco will bite. Jaco is ducking and opens his beak. I warn them look with your eyes, not your fingers. All fingers pull back starring at Jaco. He enjoys the attention with his head up. He whistles and cries like a baby. The crowd is excited. More kids join us, to see Jaco. I felt the circus came to town. I can't get off my bike. I was surrounded from excited kids talking, laughing, pushing to see my parrot. I wave to the street vendor to come over and sell me peaches. He was delighted. Jaco was the star, showing off. Spreading his tall, spread his wings pacing back and forth on the handlebar performing. We managed to get on driving, slaloms through the mountains higher and higher. The high desert scares me. No vegetation. Jokingly I say to Jaco. We reached the moon. Along came another toll station. I stop. Enter his booth. Where are you coming from? He asks unhappy leaning over his newspaper. Rio Acero, I replied friendly. Have a nice trip, he says. It is already dark when we arrive in Sucre, dirty tired and exhausted. Looking like a pig after a mud bath. No one took notice. I stopped to ask a student for a motel. He showed me a gated motel with a inner patio and a fountain. Your bike is safe there. It was clean and nice. I was glad and watch my bike closely.

Wednesday morning I go to the train station to buy a ticket. It was recommend to me. The mountains could have snow and ice. I stand in line for three hours

America: Final Destination

to buy a train ticket. A thin woman sells empanadas filled with veggies. The best I ever ate. She sold them quickly. From here I visited the museum independencia. I learned their history. In 1825 Bolivia become independent and democratic. It had war with Chile, in 1879 lost it's coastal access to Chile. Spanish with oriental influx came to Bolivia. In Potosi they made silver coins and shipped them to Spain, England and France. The French brought their culture and cuisine until 1982 they had student exchanges. Then the military came to power. They loaned money from the Swiss banks. They encouraged people to go out and buy western goods. Then came the recession, people are now struggling to make ends meet. People are hungry. I continued to the museum university to see the folklore, old pictures and old ceramics. I meet a good guide. He tells me more history and current economics. Argentina has a trade agreement with Bolivia. Argentineans first president was born in Bolivia. He promoted to have pipelines of oil going overland to Argentina. Lots of industrial goods come from Argentina.

    Jaco spent his day on the patio entertaining the wash woman. She washes all day by hand. It was afternoon, when I returned to the hotel. Two men are inspecting my bike. I watch from a distance then walked slowly towards them. I ask carefully, anything wrong with the bike? Stunned, both stare at me. The taller man breaks the silence, speaking in a business voice. I offer you two kilo of cocaine for your bike. I thought, my ears were playing a game and said shocked, could you please repeat the question? My face felt pale. The ice was broken with a smile he explains in Cochabamba you exchange cocaine for cars. I protested. I don't drive well on two kilo cocaine. Both laughed at me. You can sell it in America! I thought, they must think I am American. I shook my head and say firm NO, you keep your cocaine I keep my bike. They were deeply disappointed and tried hard to change my mind. I don't like to travel by bus. I like my freedom. They understood that. They explained how cocaine was made.

The next day I stroll the market. An amazing big variety of fresh, dried fruits and nuts that goes on forever. I fall in love with the country. I enjoy watching the farmers (campesinos) in their tradional clothing. Their antic Spanish looking hats. Their faces signed from the hard life with high cheekbones and dark skin. Everyone has a little woven bag hanging over their shoulder, filled with coca leaves. It's amazing, live TV. I am daydreaming. I see two farmers in rough clothes. They remind me of German potato sacks, their Spanish helmets, only in sandals strolling the isles. They stop by a lady. In front of her is a huge black plastic bag. They start talking to her, but I couldn't hear them. I was to far away. She holds a pantyhose in the air. Then puts both hands inside stretching and turning it. The men start to giggle and talking to each other. One claps the other on the shoulder. It was hilarious, They may never have seen a pantyhose before. The woman keeps talking with her back towards me one mans face get serious. Is she giving them now sex education? I try to take a picture of them, I get closer to get a good shot. They notice me. They put their heads down cover their faces and walk quickly away. They don't want to be photographed. I respect that, but I wished could a got a picture. I was disappointed in myself not to be fast enough. The train is scheduled to leave at 3pm. I go to drop of my bike at the depot for the cargo wagon. The men were friendly. Jaco cheered them up, by talking, laughing at them, while we waited in their warm office for the delayed train. At 5pm the office closes. We have to wait now at the platform. It was hard to say goodbye. We sit in the cold on the bench waiting. We made acquatences with a lady and her two kids, we wonder when will the train come. It's 7pm when the train arrives, cold and stiff we

America: Final Destination

hurry inside to capture a cabin for us. The boy sits next to me. He amazes me with his knowledge. The train stops in Potosi. Here is the coin museum. I wished I could visit it. Potosi is known for a typical pastry, with lots of eggs, little flour, little butter, little salt, made to a tough dough. Let it rest for a day, then bake it. It raises high, then covered with a sugar glaze. In Oruro there are hot springs, thermal water. It's good for drinking and bathing. I missed out on that, too. We see many lamas, shepherds just a few cows. We pass through gorges, valley's. It is a fascinating, amazing sights, picturesque river, green meadows, ducks and seabirds swimming in beautiful big lakes. I watch dream fully. Jaco is in his Pet carrier in the overhead department. His feathers standing up listening to the children. A baby starts crying. Jaco takes the opportunity to join in. The baby across from us stops. Many eyes start searching for the other baby. It was quit for a moment. Kids get up looking and wondering. Jaco looks down, observing the tension. To get their attention, He starts crying nonstop. One girl shouts excited, un loro (a parrot). Where, all the kids question. The girl points to the head department. All the kids come running together to see Jaco. Jaco gets quiet, looks happy at the crowd, like saying. I succeeded I have their attention. He started talking and whistling. The kids bored from the long trip found their entertainment. They pestered me to bring him out, to pet him. I shook my head, no he bites. The kids brought endless peaches, cooked corn for jaco, he enjoyed it and stayed quiet. In the morning the train stops. Local vendors come to the window. Others walk inside the train offering hot tea or selling food. The higher we got the less vegetation. I turned to the mom, wondering from what are these people live. Quietly, she says the train. Wow. In the afternoon we approach New La Paz in the background is a huge snow capped mountain with a beautiful sunset. We overlook old La Paz. The city looks like a tea kettle, in the valley. I ask her if she would know of a motel? She offers me to stay with her family tonight. It is a very dangerous at night, especially alone. We arrive at the train station, her smiling husband awaits us. He looks happy. My luggage and Jaco goes with their car. The night is bitter cold. I have difficulties to start my bike. Finally after many tries, the engine starts, I follow the car to a gated parking lot. Two German shepherds are in charge. We pay a small fee and walk uphill to their home. They live in the basement of a round tower on a hillside. It's amazing how they live. It's a small apartment as we enter my mouth drops, how modern they are. A TV in every room. The boy and the girl have their own bedroom with a TV. We sit at the table to drink tea and talk. The husband is always smiling. He works for radio carreras, his wife is a teacher. He knows Bolivia like his pocket, due to ten years of traveling the country. Now his wife tells him from my trip. She wishes she had done the same before having children. My mouth dropped open, deeply impressed from her statement. Jaco gets covered with a thick blanket for the night. In the morning, we have tea, chat and exchange addresses. Mr. Arana advises me to drive over Copacabana. That's a short cut. I thank them for their hospitality. The morning is cold, I cover jacos cage to keep him warm. La Paz is a huge city with copper stones. My engine dies several times at the stop signs while driving uphill. I have a very hard time to get the engine started, and balanced on the copper stones. On one occasion a young man suggest, acting cool. Rest and go in to have a beer. He will watch my bike. Frustrated I tell him, give me a hand and stop pestering me. I don't want a beer now. I knew he wants to steal my bike, while I sit inside drinking a beer. That trick doesn't work for me. The engine just wouldn't start, the road was slippery. He swarmed around me like a mosquito. More upset, I started pushing the bike uphill to get rid of the guy. You can't imagine how much power you

America: Final Destination

have when you are angry. I told the guy to shut up. I huffed and puffed like a steam engine. Pushing the bike uphill. Motivating myself to just get away from this guy. He finally gave up. I was ignoring him. On the top of the hill came asphalt. Hurray we made it, I say aloud so Jaco could hear me. I was soaked in sweat, a fresh breeze was blowing. I take a several deep breaths, to start the engine. After several tries it did. I stop for gas and off to Copacabana. The road was bad. The rain had destroyed the asphalt. I pay for the toll road to drive now along the famous Titicaca lake. What a wonderful feeling. With a boat I set over for the other side, the boatpeople look frightened. I wonder why? On the other side they were friendlier and ask me. Where are you from? They capture my heart, I continue on the mountain. At a police station, he asks for my passport. Show it to him. Charmingly, the young policeman asks. I like you with your long hair better, he flirts with me while writing slowly in his book. A civilian enters the room, tells him firmly to get on his post. He apologizes to me and hands my passport back, with a smile, wishing me a good trip. I travel the gorges, another control station. He asks for my driver license and explains the way. The Copacabana comes in sight, a beautiful sight. Terraces with flowers, trees a colorful paradise. Probably the rich live here. A small dreamful town, with an historic church. I visit the church and buy postcards. Send one to my friend Vivian from Bolivia living in Rio de Janeiro, married to a German. Greetings from Copacabana, Bolivia to your Copacabana in Brazil. I thought that is funny. I was deep in my thoughts, when a young Peruvian came to see Jaco. He always attacks people. We chat it is unusual to see a parrot at this altitude. We are traveling. I could have stayed here. Its so beautiful. It is around noon, now comes the scary part, leaving Bolivia, dealing with customs, immigration. Ok. I park the bike and take a deep breath as I enter the office. Surprisingly, no one was there. So I waited, after a minute a young officer dashed into the office, like chased from a swarm of bees. Out of breath, he asks angrily. Where is the bike driver? Calmly I say. I am here, where have you been? He takes a seat, looks through my passport, stamps it. I thanked him and hurried out the door, wondering. What will be next? A few meters down the street comes the customs office. I parked my bike calmly. I take a few deep breaths, pray for good luck, then enter the office. Just one officer was present. With a good feeling I approach him. I show him my passport. Where is your entry stamp, he asks disturbed? Frustrated I point it out. No your title for your bike? I don't have one, I say firmly. He looks angry at me. We get engaged in a big discussion. He insists to see the title or transit paper for my motorcycle. I have neither one. You can't leave without it. Angry, frustrated I show him my buyers contract. I explain calmly in Paraguay hardly anyone has a title. He looks the document over, mumbles something, I couldn't understand. Then he says I have to show this to my boss. He is on lunch right now. I didn't want to wait for his boss. Upset I say listen I drove through the whole country and entered without these papers. Why don't you, let me go? Over there Peru is calling me. He gets a little tender, the Peruvian customs will take your bike away. No, I protested. No, no one will take my bike. I was reaching again for my passport, he held on firm, tight. After a quiet moment, he finally gave me my passport and buyers contract back. Without hesitation I hurried out of the office, stuffed the papers in my jacket pocket. Just getting away as fast as possible was on my mind. The bike would not start, several times I try no luck. Hurriedly I push it uphill. Just be out of sight and out of mind, I think fearful. A few meters later I try again, the motor started right away. A big stone gateway framed the border. Relieved I drove through it. On the other hand my heart was heavy. I fell in love with the countryside, it is so rural and pretty. I admire the educated, caring people I met. Left my heart behind. Now I was driving in neutral zone before getting to Peru. What will be next I wonder?

Driving through Paraguay - Bolivian Chaco with thick bushes

Bolivian mountain on the road to Sucre.
Jaco on the handlebar chewing on my cables

Bolivian farmer in traditional clothing with his donkey

Passing through a mountain village.
Jaco on the handlebar

Crossing of one of many rivers on the road to Sucre through the mountains and rain forest

Baking bread in Rio Acero

PERU

There is hardly any border. A couple of buildings and a huge parking lot. I was lost, where should I go? Not a single soul so I decided to enter the biggest building with mixed emotions. A young friendly officer greeted me, like an old friend. He was so polite. I was in shock, could hardly grasp the difference from one country to the other. He was more interested to find out, where I intended to go and how. What road I intend to use and then asked for my passport. I thought I was on a different planet. I caught myself and smiled back to him. Honestly I had no clue, what road to take. He caught that. He gave me a thorough explanation, and showed me the road map on the wall. I was just overwhelmed from his friendliness. All I knew was that I wanted to go to Cusco, the ancient Inca ruins. As I smiled, he got more friendly when he learned I drove on a bike. I thought I wouldn't make it out of his office. Politely I say, it's getting late and it's a long drive to Puno. I promised him to buy a roadmap of Peru. He wished me a safe trip, but don't forget to see customs in the other building. My smile disappeared. I went to see him. He hardly looked at my papers, I was relieved and again hurried out to get back to driving again. Away from all these people and rules. The sun was shining, but it wasn't warm and a fresh wind blew. It felt so great to drive along the famous Titcacalake high in the mountains. A green valley, mountains on the left, the lake on the right. In the shade it was very cold. I passed a few villages lining the road, locals starring at me. I just waved, continued driving. Around 5pm I arrived in a bigger city, hustling, bustling, lots of people offering their goods aggressively. They have their whole arm covered with watches, gum, you name it. It was a circus. I drove slowly looking for a hostel or motel. I was always surrounded by vendors, aggressively wanting me to buy their junk. Finally I just yelled, I need a motel for the night, do you have one? The crowd disappeared. Except one. One young man helped me and guided me through the traffic. Loud music and advertisements coming from every direction. I got nervous, after the third try, we found a motel room to take my bike inside.I thanked him. I was exhausted from the turmoil. I Shared a room with two ladies from Uruguay. We go together to the dinner of their choice. The food was terrible. As we talked young locals joined us on the table. They advise me to take the train to Cusco. The road is very bad, leave your motorcycle here. Sure, I said sarcastically, when I come back I'll have two. I don't want to go the same road twice. I am going north. Again they warn me off the bad road. I thank them for their advice.

In the morning while loading my bike, the owner comes to me advising me to be careful, there are lots of eyes out there. Downtown is a chaos, bicycle taxis (rickshaws), cars coming coming from every direction, everybody just drives. I drive defensively to avoid accidents. You need eight eyes. It feels like China. It was a fiasco. Being careful and alert I look out for criminals and navigate through the city. I was glad to reach the edge of town, peaceful and quiet I approach a road barrier. The guard asks rudely. Where are you going? To Cusco I answer excited. Moody he continues the road is very bad, you won't make it. I wasn't changing my mind, he realizes it and opens the barrier. Soon the asphalt road turns into a dirt road, which was fine with me. A little bit later the road ended with a huge gravel pile. I stop and look around confused, where did the road go, I wondered? To the right is the lake, to the left is lake. I Look over my shoulder, the road runs right into the gravel mountain. Well this road needs work. I am not going back. Well, I'll just drive over the hill. Nervous, I drive to the top just to see another hill, then another. I am nervous, but I can't stop. The hills are so close together. I have to throw my heart ahead and follow. No emotion, just drive. Hill, valley, hill. On top of a hill I see another hill it seems never ending. To my right the beautiful lake Titicaca opens up. I see a couple men in a long boat cutting grass in the lake, then pulling it into the boat. They starred at me like an alien. Yes, I think I lost my mind, but I have to continue. By looking at them I nearly kissed the ground. That scared me. From now on I'll stayed focused. After ten hills or more the road appeared. I was so happy. The cross country is over. My happiness didn't last long, the road turned into a ripped washboard. I sped up to get the tense drive behind me. It turned into hours. The vibration made me tired and very thirsty. I just couldn't take it anymore, I needed a break and shifted down. My bike slides across the road like it was black ice. I fly through the air and land with my face down in the middle on the dusty, ripped road. It took me a minute to realize what happened. I got up wiped the dust of my helmet shield to see. Where is my bike? It wasn't next to me. Shocked and panicked my eyes searched for the bike. It was over there in the ditch about 3 meters away. It was leaning sideways in the ditch. Hurriedly I get over there, to avoid losing more valuable gas. It was easier said then done. I held it upright while trying to get it out of the ditch. The heavy luggage pulled it down. I was soaked to the bone from sweat. All efforts were fruitless. All a sudden I hear a motor in a distance, I listen. It came closer and closer. A pickup truck appeared with a long dust cloud behind him. Two men jump out, without saying a word, they helped me to get my bike back on the road. I was so relieved a gift from heaven. Now standing with my bike on the road, shaking the dust off my clothes, the breeze dries my sweat. The men inquired, how did it happened? I tell them my story. It will be another kilometer of this road and tunnel, then the road gets good. I was shaking and thanked my helpers and wanted to walk, but decided to just drive slower. I didn't realize how fast I was driving, before I crashed. After they left. I remember a man in the ditch leaning on the hillside. He was dressed in colorful clothing. He may have been drunk and tired from walking and fell. Did these men help him, I wondered? Hope he doesn't get a ticket for wrongful parking. The mountains gave way to beautiful green valleys and huge lama stud farms. A dreamful sight. I imagined to live here in this loneliness, if it wouldn't be so cold. It seems to be a harsh life, you can tell on these people faces. About midday I pass through a small town. Two police officers cross the street and they stop me. I got nervous. One asks for my passport. I handed to him, he opens the passport turning page by page looking. You don't have a visa, you must return to Puno to get one. I got furious. I am not driving one meter back and I get a stamp, when I entered. Nervous he looked through my passport, where? He says annoyed. Let me show you, I reached for my passport while sitting on my idling bike, but he lifted his hands with my passport. It comes to me he possibly can't read. You have to go back to Puno, he says again. I refused. Follow me. I follow him on my idling bike, while the second police stayed back, watching. I felt uneasy and trapped. I have to get my passport back. How?, after a few meters he turns around harassing me more. Asking more questions I didn't give in and sat glued to my bike, which irritated him. Their plan didn't pan out. Finally he asks do you have a souvenir or something memorable of you? I told him to close his eyes. He did. What do you see? Nothing. That's what you get I say humorously, he opens his eyes and laughs. I laugh with him. Do you have a picture of you? I think for a moment. The only one I have is in my passport and I can't tear it out. He laughs again. Hands me my passport and wishes me a good trip. I put my passport away and speeded off to the open road, promising to myself not to stop for a policeman again.

That afternoon brought more frustration, the road was full of potholes a very rough road. My luggage shifted to one side and pulled down. It seemed every half hour I had to stop and rearrange and retie the bags. The straps are cut from retired inner tubes. I was very upset and annoyed about wasting so much time. I just wanted to give up. I sat next to the road and cried, but that didn't help. My nervous were shocked, nothing helped. I took deep breaths and looked at the beautiful scenery. Grateful to be here and see it. I remember the men telling me of the bad road. I motivated myself and said just drove slower, but I continued. I need to make it to Cusco before night.

A major road barrier forced me to stop. Several military personnel stared at me, checking my passport and asking me where are you going. They actually were cool and gave me some advise and told me of the detour in town. Confused I looked ahead, where? Just follow these trucks, he said smiling. The detour road was a challenge. Did they dry the river for the detour? While they worked on the road I wondered. Only in Peru. Anything is possible. I followed the trucks during the long stretch. Finally we came to a big plaza in the center of the town. It turned into a big parking lot of trucks and Gas Riggs to stop to take a break. I saw a group of people standing, curiously I approach them. It started to drizzle. They looked at me and walked away to a church. One lady from America explained they are missionaries. Their harassing and brain washing the people, I said sarcastically. I got a dirty look. We stood in church waiting for the rain to stop. It eased, I will continue, there is lots of water in the street, you can't travel she says. I look at her puzzled what do you mean? there is lots of water in the street, I don't see any. I turned around and left. All afternoon that went through my head. The sun started to go down, I couldn't see the city. Frustrated I continued driving in the dark as it got colder the higher in elevation as we drove. I came around a corner and see in the distance streetlights. It looked so close, but we had to drive in a half circle along the mountains, the higher we came the colder it got. Finally we reached the orange streetlights, a wide asphalt boulevard my heart jumped from joy. Jaco we are almost there. Excited I drive faster to reach town, then came a sign Cusco 10 km, I was disappointed and almost alone on the road. I just wanted to get there. I reached downtown with limited street lights and not a single soul. At a bus stop, I see people and ask for directions. What's the address? Could you pull the paper out of my backpack pointing behind me? My hands are frozen. The soldier gets it out and gives me directions. Then asks could I ride with you? astonished I ask him, where? In the back,he smiles you can run behind me like the soldier in Puno. I drove away fast. On the plaza de armas I ask again for direction. It is dark and spooky. One woman pleads to my ear be careful with your luggage and your bike. I understood. I drive around the plaza into the side street. It was a dark night with barely any light. Its creepy and mysterious. I drove slow on Copper stone streets lined with stonewalls on both side. Like in medieval time. I felt uneasy. I wondered is this the right way? I came around the corner and see a couple young guys, I stop and ask again for direction, one speaks fluent German. They offer to guide me to the motel asking a lot of questions in the process, I wasn't in the mood. Are you a policeman? The streets feel like a labyrinth and creepy. We pass more drunks asking for money, we come around another corner and I see a big Iron gate with the sign " Bolivar" enough from panhandlers, I jump on my bike and drive directly into the hallway. A few men look at me with an open mouth. One approached me. Do you have a bed, I ask? We have no vacancies. I get upset and pass on the greetings from a person in Puno, stating you have a bed. He thinks, we have one in the back, it is not so nice. I didn't care, but I did ask for help with my luggage and bike. The boys helped me. We walked through long dark hallways, upstairs, downstairs, around some corners. In the last corner was the room. We left the bike in the hallway. Your bike is safe here, said the boy. We overlooked now a inside patio, like a mission, across is the bathroom and showers. I thanked him. Relived, I put my bag in a simple room with a bed. I took care of Jaco, he was all day locked up in his cage. I walk slowly downstairs stiff and sore awaiting for a long hot shower, so I could defrost my bones. After ten minutes or so life came back to my body little by little. Today I didn't care about water conservation. Warm and clean I return to my small room. I ate a can of tuna with some bread thinking of my father. Today is his birthday, I mailed him a card. I crawled, totally exhausted under the warm heavy blankets, thinking about my day. I drove 396 kilometer on horrible roads. People had warned me about the bad road, but the breathtaking views and valleys made up for it. If I had less luggage driving would have been easier, but I needed everything I packed. For a long time I couldn't sleep. I prayed to god to give me the strength to continue. I am on the bottom of the map until I reach America. Will I make it? Who knows at this point.

  On February 23rd I wake up refreshed. What a difference last night made. A little sore I fead Jaco and take off to the train station on foot to buy an advanced train ticket to Macho Pitchu It is a long wait, definitely in high demand. From here I visited the Indian market with many handcrafts and typical clothing. Everyone encourages me to buy from the streets. Its overwhelming. I settle for a for a small hand woven bag while always standing in the sun to get warm. I stop at a travel agency for a map. He has only a wall map. Which is the shortest way to Lima from here, I ask. His smile disappeared He warns me of the terrorists, don't take the direct route from Cusco to Lima. The terrorists will attack you, rape you, and steal your bike. He let the air out of me. You are safer going back to Puno. That didn't excite me. Frustrated, disappointed, I left his office and still had no map of Peru. I checked the train prices to Puno. For my bike they asked a ridiculous price. We debated for a long time they wouldn't change their mind. I will drive back. One suggested in Pisca you could take the road to the coast. I thanked them on the way out, I meet a German speaking Peruvian. We talk and go for dinner to a small cozy restaurant. They served wood fired pizza and spaghetti. We sit with other germans talking and have a good time. We listened to a four man band and local music. It was the best band I ever had heard. Afterward we went to a disco, the four man band came in to play their Andean music. It was a great night out. On February 24th I took a train trip to Machu Pitchu. I was very excited. The train was packed with locals and their goods and tourist mixed, I couldn't see much. The train moved than it stopped. I hear rattling we get shaken. Then the train moved again, the wrong way. Confused I look around. What is going on? I asked one German. He explained the whole process, how the train goes back and forth, in zigzag, because the mountain is so steep. I didn't have a clue till now. I found a seat, I got stomach cramps, and couldn't enjoy my day to the fullest. We reach the top and the train stopped in every town. Kids offered, filled potatoes, cooked corn, a driving market. The air was filled with all sort of unpleasant odors. The woman carry their kids wrapped in a cloth on their back. They nurse their babies in public, its natural. Often you get an elbow in the back or a basket is on your head. A simple, humble excuse me and shuttle their way through the mess. I continued sitting, because my stomach cramps wouldn't go away. At one station a woman picks up a bag from the floor, oink oink, little piglets! No wonder it stinks in here. I was in a bad mood due to pain. In Machu Pitchu lots of people get off the train. I look around wondering. Where are the ruins? We are in a valley with a mighty big river called Urubamba. Across the street is a long line I get in line. Curious I ask the person in front of me, is this the way to Machu Pitchu? Unfriendly he answers, are you here to buy a ticket for the minibus? I felt like an idiot and have no idea. Two young guys behind me smile, are you alone? Yes, I say surprised. Would you like to come with us? So you are not alone. O.k. They explain every few minutes a bus leaves to the ruins. We get on a minibus he drives zig zag up the mountain on a paved road. My neighbor sitting next to me from Israel speaks German. He belongs to a group of retirees. They fly from one sightseeing tour to the other in south America. This must be expensive, I commented We worked all of our lives. On the top my new friends waited for me. Juan, Velto. Again we stand in line for tickets. I look at the chart Tourist pay 100% more, that's amazing. You are my wife if they ask and gave him the money. He paid for me admittance to the ruins. We all laughed, so fast you could get married, for five minutes only. In front of us are the ruins. Its breathtaking. In this altitude to build a town and have fields. Together we walk the ruins, I wonder about the architecture so long ago, so fascinating. They knew little about their history. From a vista point you can see the Inca bridge, in reality a small path hammered into the granite rock. It goes straight up and straight down. You couldn't make a mistake, walk like a goat. You had to be dizzy free. To cross the wooden bridge over a valley. The narrow bridge looked like two two by fours. These messengers were amazing. I get sick just by looking. I go a couple steps back. The morning frost is still on the ground, afraid to slide down the mountain. It is impressive how the Incas lived, worked and built thousands of years ago. On another site the terraces are clearly defined, where they had fields, deep down is the wild brown river Urubamba running. Here meets the world, I met a couple from California, Hillsborough, they knew the Stevens. Wow. I am on my way to visit them. How small is the world. I felt great for a moment. In the afternoon the train returns to Cusco. Two soldiers stayed on the train for protection. Terrorists are out there, they said. Juan, Velto are very friendly, inviting me to their home. I didn't want to be questioned, asking me ten thousand questions by their family. I Preferred to buy food in the store, and go back to the hotel. The kids came running telling me their wonderful day with Jaco. Surprisingly he was already in his cage. He commented about his day, I was relieved. Quickly I go to bed. The next morning I didn't want to to get up. It was a cold cloudy day, but I have to continue. The bike didn't start. The rest didn't do good to the motor. A taxi driver, was trying to give me advise, asking me more questions. He just irritated me, and finally I got the motor started. It was a great deal. I asked for the way to Pisca. Surprisingly the road was good, what happened? They fixed the road. In San Juan (Sicuani) at a road barrier stood two soldier smiling at me. You are coming back? Aren't you? I tell them the horror stories, I was told. Not to drive straight from Cusco to Lima, due to the terrorists. As we talk, one of them says, you have nice blue eyes. Thank you, but there are not for sale, I said laughing. An old soldier comes and joins our conversation. There is a shorter way to Arequipa, he explains. Pointing straight ahead. When you come to a big rock, turn right. I was very relieved and thanked him. They wanted to keep me. In Peru the men are behind me, in Bolivia they were after my bike. Happy I go on the short cut, shortly after the road looks like a plowed field, with rocks and potholes, I tell Jaco don't learn my swearing words. I was so angry, but continued driving looking at the beautiful mountain ridges lining the way. Rock formations like in Arizona made up for the bad road, Tourists don't come here Its been overcast all day. After hours of driving, I stop at an intersection in the afternoon, asking two men for directions. They recommended that I stay the night in the upcoming village. He continues talking about the robberies and assaults happen that happen around here. I found it exaggerated, but stayed in Yauri. Surprisingly the people were friendly and I found an hostel easily. As always, I had my bike inside and Jaco sat on a chair for the night. I walk around town to stretch my feet. On a corner stands a woman with a cart. Curious I approach her. Two men stood by her, each of them holding a glass in their hand. I asked the woman what do you have for sale? Tea, she said. I buy a glass and look inside her big pot, I see quince and herbs. In Germany we make jelly from quince. It tastes very good, it warms you up. The evening is cold. I crawled under my blankets and go to sleep. Jaco didn't seem to be bothered by the cold like I was. I hear a knocking on my door, I open it a bit, there is that guy again. Angry I tell him, to leave me alone. I paid for the bed, not for company. I slammed the door in front of his nose, and that was the third time. To avoid another visit, I went to the owner to complain. He just listened, which made me even more mad. If this guy comes again, I'll go to the police. I turned on my heel and left. He never came back. In the morning everybody was respectful, asking me, where are you going? Arequipa. It is very far. Do you go alone?, she asks surprised. I have my parrot. Do you have enough warm clothes? I showed her my long johns, socks, two pullovers, one T-shirt, one A shirt, leatherjacket and gloves. She didn't answer and I thanked her for her concerns. I drove off into the lonely mountains. Here I feel safe, not threatened. Nobody bothered me or tried to steal something. I love it out here, beautiful mountain ranges, and winding roads. The morning sun is coming up, I dream into the day, driving with one eye on the road, the other eye on the scenery. The roads splits, I stop it feels so chilly. Jaco is in his cage, covered with a wax tablecloth, to keep him warm. I look for the sun, I have to go north. I decided to go right. I saw a bicycle coming. One young man was sitting on the fork, the other peddling. I ask for directions, they point straight ahead. Shortly after I came to a road barrier with a little home. A middle aged man stands at the door smiling. I ask, how far is it to Arequipa, casually he says, in six hours you'll be there. I was so happy. Ready to take off, he says wait, wait there is the guard. A man approached us fast. He asks lots of questions. Aren't you cold? I am alright, however I am not getting warmer by standing here. It got colder and more questions followed. Finally I was fed up, and said a friend awaits me in Arequipa then he lets me go, I was very relieved, I had no patience to be entertained. The scenery was naked, very rocky and lots of stones. At a distance came another road barrier, he checks per radio with the last guard then he asks for my passport, I could hear his voice. Yes a foreigner with a red bike came through. A few minutes later he lets me go. It got considerably colder, I think about the words the first guard said and understood now, what he meant, but I had no choice. Don't look back, only foreword, forcing myself to continue. It got even more colder, I started to feel like a popsicle, I could hardly move my fingers. Cold air blew into my clothing. I forced myself to drive. I pass a few dump trucks, wondering, what are they doing in this god forbidden world? There is hardly any vegetation. The road is at times narrow, windy, uphill. Surprisingly, later came several trucks in sight, I passed one after another. They drove to slow for me. The road went constantly uphill, I clearly felt the air getting

America: Final Destination

thinner and the motor loosing power. I think about the German guy in Chaco, he thought my bike wouldn't run in the thin air. Why did he worry? He wasn't going with me. He was going with his consul back to Asuncion. I am on my way north, and I had to prove him wrong. That conversation passed through my mind.

Two trucks were driving close together, several times I tried to pass them. They wouldn't let me. I always had to shift down, I got angrier and angrier. In a curve I took my chance in my hand passed both trucks on loose gravel, with sharp stones. They tried to push me off the road. They were plain mean and I could feel them. In desperation I gave more gas to get passed them. I had taken a big chance. Then I heard an unpleasant sound and got a bad feeling, but leaving the trucks behind. After a while I needed to check on my rear tire. It didn't feel right. At a plateau I stopped I could hardly move. It was freezing cold. My body was a solid ice cube. I look down a flat tire. That is what I needed. Stiff from the cold, I get up and push. The tire wabling. I can't do this, it will ruin my tire. Depressed, I stood there thinking of what to do. I walk to the next town? Who knows how far that could be? I decided to wait for a truck. I look after Jaco, he is angry about the cold. He lays flat at the bottom of the cage. I could understand. After a while came the trucks I had passed. I stood in the middle of the road waving. They passed me. Later came another one, I wave at him. He stopped in a distance he looks at me, I go to him explaining my situation. He has an air pump? He was in a T shirt! I couldn't believe it. We pump up the tire, this should hold you until town, he says grumpy. I thanked him, after a few kilometers my tire was flat again. Angry I wait for him again, it seemed forever. We pumped up the tire again. After the third time I ask him humbly, could you take me to the next town? Instead of stopping every kilometer? That gets old very quickly. He was very concerned, not thrilled. I took my helmet off. His face changed. A woman! We waited for another truck to come and help us to load the motorcycle into the dump truck, which was a real challenge. Jaco went right away into the cabin. To get warm. While I stood with teeth chattering, waiting for the two trucks. They stopped in a distance, greeting each other. At first they had to tell jokes. Where is the TV from the back of the motorcycle? It is not a TV, it is a animal cage with a parrot inside. Where is he? In the warm cabin. Finally they helped. We tied the bike up, to keep it from falling. I hurried to the truck cabin. Jaco hangs on the side of the cage. He is confused. The cabin is warm and cozy. Now I understand why the guys wear T-shirts. Slowly my bones defrosted and over time I peeled my clothes like a banana. At about 11 am we have lunch at a house next to the road. The owner asks the driver, where did you pick her up? At cinco de mayo with a flat tire and she has a parrot with her. The owner was speechless for a moment and turned to me. This is the highest point of the road 5 500 meter high, as he shakes his head at me. We eat rice, goat meat, onion, green salad, beer and coke. It feels great to be on top of the world. The owner recovers and says you are lucky. We have no snow today. You like the food? Yes I do. People are marked from the harsh environment. He stays in business from the truckers, stopping for warm food. We continue driving the famous Andean mountains on windy roads. I took pictures of the most beautiful rock formations. It just fascinates me with so much and to see, and it with my own eyes. We pass herds of lamas, but more alpacas (bauhinias) a smaller breed of lamas with fine wool. It gets exported to America. The lama wool is useless, but the meat tastes good. Time flies, we arrive in a tiny village, several homes are abonded or collapsed. We stop in front of an adobe house, where a woman sells basic goods. The driver buys cans of tuna and gives them to me. I ask for the mechanic. Where is his shop? Slowly, silently she points across the street. The home is abonded, she nods. Where is the mechanic?, I ask surprised. He may come in two or three days or even a week, whenever he feels like it according to his routine. My heart slips in my shoes. I don't want to gamble, sit here until the mechanic shows up. I approach the driver, where are you going to the mechanic? Yes, could I go there? He gets nervous, my boss will get angry. I will explain my situation to him my situation. He thought about it and finally agreed to take me to his camp and train station. Gladly I go with him. Leaving the ghost town behind and a church without a roof in the high desert. Now he warms up and tells me in Tintaya is a big mine. there digging for minerals and some Gold. Export the minerals to Canada. Peru's national flag is red and white. About five pm we arrive in camp. On the left is a big fenced area, with a big metal building, the workshop. Across the street are a few shacks, I wait at the gate. He drives in, asks a few men to unload the bike and fix the flat tire. Helpless, they stand around my bike looking at each other. What are they waiting for I asked the guard? Would you let me talk to them? He allowed me to go to my bike. What is going on? One mechanic says I work only on trucks, I turn to another mechanic, could I have some tools? I will do it myself. No, no. we will fix it and was ordered to leave. From across the street I watch helpless, the mechanics starring at my bike. The woman and her kids start talking to me. Times passes, I get nervous, wondering what are they doing? I couldn't believe it they don't know how to take the tire off. From time to time the driver came over, I asked is my bike fixed? No, I watched five or six men trying to get the tire off. I was infuriated. I could've done it faster myself and was ready to explode. Hours go by, they managed to take the tire off. It started to get dark. The driver talked to the woman cross the street about accommodating me in her tin shack. I still wondered, where is the town? Where is my luggage and Jaco? Across the street, he says. Worried and frustrated I walk over there. She already covered Jaco in his cage for the night. It is a risk to bring him to this climate. Relieved I thanked her. The driver made arrangement with the woman and her six kids for me to stay the night. She shows me a humble a bunk bed nailed together with two by fours from left over construction wood. You sleep on the top, we sleep on the bottom. I protested one can sleep with me, three people in a bed is to tight. No, it is OK. A man comes to the door, come to dinner, orders from the boss. We all look at each other, see you later. We walk against a strong blowing wind. We enter another Tin shack, it is very small, but cozy. Curtains divide the room. I come to the table, I share a wood bench with the men we sit close together, keeping each other warm. A woman comes from the kitchen with a plate of food, chicken, tomato and rice. It was very good. I could have ate two plates. Carefully I ask the boss, is my tire fixed? Yes, it is finished, he answered irritated. A miracle happened, I couldn't hold back, these are Indians. A huge discussion started, the boss replied again, just be happy. It is done. I was happy. The boss criticized me. When I go on a trip, I take maps, brochures, make reservations, everything is in order, all planned. Not just like a shot in the dark. I listened to him smiling, this is alright. If I had not had a flat tire, I would be now in Arequipa at a reserved room and the best maps you pick up in each country. A voice from the dark agreed with me. We sat for hours, tight together like a sardines in a can talking I have good time. The boss was very uptight. Poor like a church mouse, but with a big heart to help each other. The woman reminds us that it is late and time to go home. We would have sat until midnight. The sky was covered with bright stars guiding me to my Hollywood motel with the health bed, I thought with humor. They let me in and fully clothed I climbed in bed. It had a lama fur on the bottom and warm blankets to cover. I have to turn slowly in bed, it was shacking I was afraid it would collapse. The howling cold wind blew through the cracks, I crawled totally under the blankets. I couldn't sleep. The wind became my music and a song went through my mind. It was a cold night. In the morning they asked concerned. Did you sleep good and were you warm enough? Yes, I did. Then I asked them for the toilet. They looked at each other quietly, I read in their eyes, there is none. The mother of nine children, each from a different father told one child to take me behind the house, pointing in the distance, there any where. The neighbor appears, sits behind a dirt pile doing her business, so I did the same. Friendly I ask the woman how much do I owe you? She said its all paid for, I thanked her and properly the truck driver paid her. I took off to get my bike. The same here, nobody would except money. I thanked them from the bottom of my heart. Then I loaded my bike to drive 99 kilometer to Arequipa. I was so excited, but the road was another washboard with black sand and gravel. It was a nerve wrecking drive, slightly going downhill. I enjoyed nature with its natural beauty. I had to stop so every often to tighten my luggage, realizing I lost my leather belt, a gift from my father. I got very upset, but didn't want to drive back, who knows where I lost it, I was devastated. Well it will be a lucky finder, somebody will need it After three hours driving appears Arequipa. Now my dreams become reality, Goosebumps go down my spine from excitement. Ahead appears the three black cone mountains reaching for the sky. Called "El misty" It was a breathtaking view. I was blown away. Nestled between the three inactive volcano lies the city Arequipa. Arequipa is a very busy city, an anthill, people are unfriendly, they don't answer questions. I won't stay here long. The hostels are very expensive or occupied. I remembered Marco advised me of a hostel, the people are unfriendly and rude. I mentioned several times his name. then she smiled, saying I have a simple room. I was relieved. In the afternoon arrived the laundrywoman, I see soap water wasted, my bike being very filthy, like from a mud bath and dust. I asked for the dirty soap water to wash my bike. She didn't mind. The clothes got clean and as well my bike, I joked with her. We laughed. This is a city in the desert. There is a water shortage you have to conserve. Jaco entertained a German couple, they were on the way to Cusco, Macho pitchu. Now is carnival time, no bus is going, they tell me with disappointment. How nice it is to have a vehicle, they envied me. You can come and go as you want. For us it is not worth to buy a vehicle for two or three weeks. I felt fortunate. A Swiss family came by bus from Ecuador, telling us how bad the road was. In the afternoon I run into Marco, what a surprise to see you, I said. A family approaches me, they saw me in Bolivia, I was speechless. We visited for a while, nice people. The hostel is very popular, meeting all these people from everywhere. The city itself has little to offer, barely any sightseeing. Due to the carnival you have to walk carefully, because water filled balloons are dropped on you or thrown at you. Several times I got an unwanted bath. A group of teenagers dropped balloons from the second floor balcony on me. They laughed as I shook the water out of my hair and laughing with them. Its carnival time of happiness. In the evening I went with Marco to the Plaza de Armas where his friend has a restaurant. He tells him about my trip, they fantasize about putting an article in the newspaper, I don't like the idea. I said I'm afraid to get assaulted and robbed or possibly my bike stolen. I preferred to travel unseen, invisible, just another traveler on the road not looking for fame. We hear the Pan-American highway is washed away from a strong rainstorm. A 100 year event. The coast rarely sees rain. They showed me the newspaper. We debated whether it would be better in Lima to get on a ship. I agreed. The next morning. I left the city. What a country?, the people in the camp are very poor but so friendly and nice. Here they are the opposite. I just wanted to go. Jaco liked the company at the hostel. He was the major attraction unloading his vocabulary and having fun.

The asphalt road leads through the desert to the coast, naked, black mountains greeting us. Jaco is in his cage in the back covered up. The area is mysterious feeling lonely, no vegetation. It's lifeless and uncomfortable to me. For hours I drove through the desert, the strong wind constantly shifting. I feel like a leaf in the wind. The sun is burning on me. Sometimes the road is straight like a candle. I see mirage, visualize lakes, water in a distance, but it is all a dream. It is nerve wrecking. Someone easily could loose their mind. I start to sing to keep my mind occupied and my sanity. The mountains come in sight again, the road gets curvy downhill. Shifting sand often covers the asphalt roads and goes into my eyes, my ears and my nose. Hours pass with no one in sight. I could smell the ocean, I was so happy to finally reach the coast. The ocean comes in sight and I see seagulls many pelicans, my heart was filled of joy. Finally water, I looked at the crashing waves I loved it, but no vegetation. In the valley is a green oasis, a river leads to the ocean. Afterwards it is desert again. Sand, strong winds the Pan-American highway is a nightmare. I wish to meet the person naming Pan-American highway the dream road of the world. I am boiling from anger. Lots of sandstorms, the sand enters my eyes so I can't see. The sunglasses and helmet visor don't help. Driving half blind for hours and hours. The trucks drive in the middle of the road, they are not moving one centimeter I avoid several head on collisions. They are not moving or staying in their lanes. I swear like a champion. I stopped at a gas station to buy gas and the guy walks away and it leaves me without words. I continue driving, he doesn't want my money. Well tourist and strangers are not welcome, I guess.

After almost twelve hours of driving I arrive in Nasca and look for a room. It is a bigger town. Tired, I find a hostel Marco recommended. It is on the first floor, it doesn't work for me. The owner refers me to another one. I remember Marco telling me to go to some history event. He doesn't understand, I don't know the city and I Haven't found a place to stay yet. I think sweating, It is well meant, but I have priorities, sorry Marco. In the hostel Ramon, the bike fits into the room, but I couldn't shower, because the water is turned off. I swear again. Peru is a crucified country, don't come here.

The president is popular, he gives a lot of money to agriculture to make the coast green. He is 36 years young, from Japan, but he doesn't spend money on the roads. The terrorists are from the last president and foreigners. Exhausted, I go to bed. I put Jaco on the back of a chair. What a wonderful friend. He has hardly complained yet, I am glad to travel alone with my parrot. I don't think a person would endure with me, like he does. I always push myself to the extreme, making the best in every situation. People often shake their head about me. Yes, Peru is a crucified land except for a few good people. They have been abused, exploited for centuries and that's where their distrust comes from.

In the morning I go to the market for food. When I return the owner says friendly. A man came looking for you. Surprised, I say. You sure, I don't know anyone. I return to my room and eat breakfast with Jaco. All a sudden Marco stands on my door, at seven am. I am speechless, my mouth dropped. How did you find me? Marco smiled, the other hostel told me. Did you go last night to the event? I responded, no I was to exhausted and don't know my way around. We talked for a while, then I took off to get my oil change done. That guy had no tools, he goes to borrow a wrench, while I wait. With these people you need nerves like iron. I talked to a Peruvian lots of sweet-talk, I just let it pass by, while he changed my oil. He delayed me a lot. Finally at eleven am I take off to Lima, later then expected. The drive is boring, 444kilometers way. My butt is tired from sitting, so I take turns sitting on the left than on the right. I see seagulls, pelicans and smell the fish from the ocean. It made me feel good, I love the ocean. The scenery changes from mountains to ocean, lots of sand, I force myself to continue to drive, finding the asphalt is more tiring.I talk to myself to stay awake. Jaco is in his cage, covered with a vinyl tablecloth. Ths is a strange area for him. I stop from time to time to check on him. Surprisingly he is in a good mood. You are my best friend. I wouldn't know of a better friend which would endure the challenges and stress with me. I pass a few man made oasis's, the water comes from the highlands to the coast and makes the desert fertile and green. I see pasture and flower plantations my heart jumps from joy. Finally life, people. The loneliness is hard. I pass nice beaches packed with people sun bathing, swimming in the lagoons. It must be family day lots of people are on the beach. A meat market otherwise I would a stay. The worst was yet to come, traffic, bumper to bumper. A metal avalanche in the afternoon. Driving 20 to 30 kilometers an hour, passing accidents, flat tires, potholes in the road. Cautiously I stay behind a car, hours of driving and the city is still not in sight. I am getting nervous The two lane road widens to to three lanes and traffic picks up. Without destination I drive through the big city looking for a hostel. The Brenda district has supposly cheap hostels. I ask several times, but people don't understand me or don't know. I am frustrated. Lost, confused I drive through the lit up city at night. Passing advertisements, cinemas, factories and companies. No hotels in sight. It gets cold and late, I stop and ask a pedestrian. He tells me his life story. He works at Pepsi and is on his way to work, impatiently I interrupt, where is the hostel? In a monotone voice he says he has no money and gives and me his phone number and four fichas to call him. I am boiling hot, where is the hostel? I don't want money from you. For a moment he looks stunned and points in a direction. Before he could close his mouth, I was gone. Still angry thinking what an idiot. I found the street, but where is the hostel? I see two men arguing and ask for a hostel. It was dark in the street and barely anyone on the road. The smaller guy was bleeding on top of his head. The hair were full of blood. the other was tall and husky. The two look frightening to me, the closer I came. I ask for a hostel. The small guy smiles right here, pointing at the door. Exhausted I ask if there is a room available for the night? No, vacancies, he declared. Disappointed I tell him for hours I have been searching for a room for my bike and I. All of a sudden he has a room, we negotiate the price. I got a big room but the bike doesn't make the corner. The room has a window facing the hallway, I find it odd. He recommends, we leave the bike in front of the window by my room. Unhappy I agree. Tired, exhausted, I sit on the bed. Suddenly I hear voices in the hallway, I rush to the window. Open a crack to see. The small guy with the bloody head, well now he has a band aid and talks to the gorilla. A big husky guy. You can tell he is not very bright. The small guy talks fast and convincing to the gorilla agreeing to everything by nodding his head. The small guy leaves, the gorilla starts displaying his muscles. The gorilla is obviously under the thumb of the small guy. I don't trust the place. When I am asleep he could easily carry my bike away, even if it was locked with a big chain. I watched him for a while, and had a bad feeling. I decided to go to the reception to ask for a different room. He was busy. Politely

America: Final Destination

I waited until he attended all other guests. He takes their I.D. opens a drawer and takes a roll of toilet paper out, while talking to the young couple. Unrolling the paper, he gives them a big chunk of it. I felt uneasy, what did I get myself into. I ended up in the three color house in Lima. Then he asks for my passport. I ask politely for another room, where my bike may fit. He's unfriendly, he looks into his book, suddenly the small guy stands next to me. What is the problem? He asks curiously. I get a new room, I explained happily. No, you don't. Your bike will be safe. Depressed I went back to my room. Jaco was already asleep. When I wanted to go to take a shower, the inside lock wouldn't turn. I was in shock. I tried and tried again. No luck, I heard voices in the hallway and, shout for help. I knock on the door. Again the small man is there. He gives me instructions on how to open the door. Nothing worked. He gets angry at me. I reply the lock is not moving. Jaco looks at me, sleepy, yawning. Can't I get any peace? Then there was silence for a while. I felt like in a prison. Then I hear a noise, where is it coming from? It comes from the corner of the room up high. There is a small thick glaswindow. It opens, there sit's the little man from James Bond (the man with the golden gun) I was stunned. There sat the small guy in the air vent, I had to laugh and ask him. Do you need help to come down? He didn't, it was to funny. Then he started fiddling with the lock. I watched him with joy, sarcastically I ask, you have a problem opening it? It is supposly so easy. He couldn't open it. He vanished through the small window to get some tools. He came back. It took him a long time to get the door open. I sat amused on the bed watching, because according to him, I am to stupid to open it. While he works on the lock, I take off for the shower. I see a tall good looking man with a towel wrapped around, like Tarzan. He sees me and wraps the towel around his body and disappears. It was amusing. Who comes around the corner? The small man again. Where is the shower? I ask him. He smiles, I'll show you, he put his arm around my hip. I protested, don't touch me like I am married to you. and, took his arm of my hips. I showered, but he couldn't get the lock fixed. Frustrated they gave me a different room. Jaco protested to be disturbed while sleeping, I tell him calmly it will be better for us. That night I slept deep. I dreamed one of their gorillas came through the small window and stole parts of my bike, I awoke rapidly. It took me a while to realize where I was. I looked around and the bike was alright. I closed the window to the hallway, but later I had more nightmares. In the morning I took the bus to the harbor in Callao. Leaving Jaco in the room behind. The bus was like a driving in a sardine can. I watched the people rushing to work. The cashier helped certain people to get in or out of the bus. How interesting. Later on the bus lightened up the cashier was sitting on the dashboard counting the money. I realized over the long trip, that he got more and more rings on his fingers. A light went on. I was glad to get off. A huge harbor was in front of me. I asked my way through. The harbor police instructs me to go to the Captains office. They know which ship is going to Panama. There I stood firm my ground to get to the right person. Not running back and forth. A smiling, tall, polite middle aged receives me. They keep you hidden, he laughs. Calm, relaxed he studies the ship records, where each ship is going. He turned many pages, finally he found one Colombian. The captains wife is German. Very nice man, a good friend of mine he said and gave me instructions. Good luck. Full of joy, I ran back to the harbor police and ask for the ship. The captain is in the city. I waited and then the police took my passport to talk to the captain. Waiting for 45 minutes or longer, I ask an officer for help. A young good looking Peruvian identifies himself as policeman. I tell him my situation, I am waiting for my passport and the captain. He looks for him, shortly after he comes back. The captain has not returned yet. Lets have a cup tea he said. I agreed. After our return, the captain had arrived. We go together to the ship to meet the captain. A tall, slim, good looking man with glasses, with a great smile. We have an honest straight talk, he said he would help me. Alone, he states that his wife is German from Hamburg. He laughs at the idea to have a parrot and a motorcycle on board. I promised to follow all the rules, I said. He shows me a officer cabin right next to his. Office. A bed with white linen, I forget how it looks high up is a round window. There was a couch, table, chair, toilet and shower by the entrance. I felt like a Queen. One concern, I wondered, is the air conditioner to cold for Jaco. The laundry room is warm, says the captain smiling. I am very impressed from the captain and so happy. He takes us on board. Go get your belongings, the captain says smiling. My dream became true, to get on a ship. The young policeman offers to come with me to the hostel. I welcome him. He will help me to get passed the harbor police to the ship. Off to the hostel, I said Surprised the staff looks at us, the small man is there, too. I greeted everyone, friendly, my companion didn't know better to show his title. A policeman from the harbor. I was embarrassed, ignorant dude. I saw a shock going through the staff's faces. What did we do? I got angry, pulled the policeman on the arm. I explained to them he accompanies me to get my stuff and to get into the harbor, their faces light up. Jaco was happy to see me. We loaded the bike, jaco and I sat in the back. It was very tight. He knows the way to the harbor, I let him drive. At the harbor we had problems to get in. You need a pass, he said. My driver stayed calm. He says there are more doors, we pass both checkpoints and make it to the ship. A stern soldier stopped me. I talk to him, explaining I just want to bring the luggage on board. He agreed after thoroughly searching my bags. He gave me a headache, I have nothing to declare. A black sailor comes to help me, both of us are angry about the militaerypolice. Jaco finally goes to the warm Laundry room. He was so happy. The day was cloudy day kind of depressing. The ship is cool and fresh. Relieved I leave the ship to get my stamp. The small policeman smiles, excuses himself for this morning, so did I, it is OK to be distrustful. You have to watch out. Meanwhile I was back to the ship, waiting…. The sailor calls the office in San Isidro to the ship agency, to hear the captain got permission for me to travel on the containership, man was I relieved. It turned out a long torturous process. Phone calls, stamps, waiting, etc. The Peruvians are a very stubborn people. They love to make people wait or try to steal everything they can from them. The captain had left the office in town. I waited impatiently for him. The captain arrives. we only look at each other. You have to get it yourself. I went back to the captain office at the harbor. What a circus, I return to the ship and the captain invites me for dinner, but to our surprise I could not stay overnight. Orders from the top, says the soldier. We were very surprised. They would have not allowed me to stay the night. We talked and talked but, nothing helped. We controlled our anger, and follow the instructions. The young police offers me to stay the night with him and his father. I deny him firmly, I stay another night in the hostel. Unhappy and disappointed we go divided ways. The hostel staff was speechless to see me again. You again? Why? I explain quickly the story and ask politely for the same room. Bored I walked the streets. A tall middle aged Peruvian invites me for a cup of coffee. I said yes, I had time to kill. We had a relaxed conversation. He looks at my hands, and says heartfelt, you work a lot, you need a vacation. I invite you for 15 days. I laugh at him. No, thank you, to late. Tomorrow I go on a ship up north. He said, stay 15 days longer, you will have a good

America: Final Destination

time. I laugh again, my luggage is on board and I am going!

Early in the morning I arrive at the ship. The captain greets me, invites me to breakfast. I see Jaco and feed him. For hours we wait nervous for the agency to give the final permission for me to become a passenger on the ship" Rio Triando." I was afraid they are changing their minds again. Suddenly I hear the captains voice, calling me. My heart slipped into my pants pocket. I ran fast to his office. Smiling, excited he stands at the window. Look they are loading your bike. A crane with long cables lifted my bike in the air. It hangs like a fly, I run to get my camera and took several pictures. Full of joy, we watch the loading of my bike. Now you don't have to be afraid anymore, says captain Uribe smiling. A big rock fell from my heart, I was relieved. At lunchtime the 12: 30 conference is over and police, agents, the captain and city clerk leave happily talking. The captain hands me my passport with an exit stamp. Happy and excited I take it from him. The frightful, nerve wrecking time is over for now any way. The Peruvians exhaust me. Peacefully I return to my cabin. Two tug boats guide us out of the harbor. One older tugboat man accompanies us. Finally we are on the ocean. I am very relieved. I spent the afternoon at the bridge. The officers explain all the instruments to me. It's very interesting. In the evening the captain invites me, to get to know his passenger to freshen up on his English. We talk about the world, countries, travel, and history. He loans me a book to pass the long hours. At four am we arrive in Chill, Peru. I have to get up at three am to be on the bridge, the captain excused himself. I went to sleep. In the morning we have officers on board. I look at them disgusted, they only bring problems. They heard a parrot is on board. The captain asks me politely to bring him. He is a great man always smiling. I get Jaco from the warm laundry room. The only warm room. I enter with jaco the captains office. Jaco greets the officer, hello Jaco. Everybody smiles, lots of questions follow, while Jaco sits on my shoulder. He bites my ear and pulls on my mouth like saying. Don't give these guys so much attention. You have me. Later the captain told me and the crew the Peruvian inspector took all their south African wine as they searched the whole ship. I could feel their pain. Later I take Jaco to the bridge, he is nervous about the new environment, seeing seagulls flying by. I keep an eye on them. Jaco entertains the officers, we fall in a conversation. I am a little shy and uncomfortable. I have never seen these officers before, and don't like long talks with strangers, but I have I try to hide it. I have lunch at the office cantina, a small mess hall, compared to the big sailor mess hall. The captains asks about my plans. I am comfortable around him. I tell him of my plans. In California I'm going to sell my bike and buy a new one. In California or Florida. I go on board of a ship to Chile or brazil. The captain smiles again. I like your ship and appreciate your help. The captain concluded from now on you eat here. I was surprised and thanked him again.

  March 5th, on Willy's birthday, I wished he would have been here, but I think it would have been harder to travel and get on board. Being alone is easier. Today I am baking cakes for the captain, he likes sweets. This is my way to say thanks to him. I made chocolate cake with raisins, and cookies. I talk a lot with the cooks to get all my ingredients. They tell me about their country Colombia. It must be beautiful. I have a song on my lips. Where are you going? I am happy to work in the kitchen and bake for the whole crew. They ask me to become a sailor, everybody loves my baking. They praise me, I continue backing, leaving nothing behind. Everybody licks their fingers from my baking. We are in a good mood, the captains voice interrupts us. Where is he? I ask. It's the loudspeaker. I run upstairs to the captains office to meet the happy, smiling captain. We have company I come to the window. We see dolphins accompanying us, jumping out of the water in front of the ship. It's a sea mans joy to see the playful dolphins. They followed us for a long time. Later we see by the coast of Peru whales. I see the whales come up, their teeth, they go under water and come up or one sees a fountain of water. We know their present. I am sure to become a seaman now, it is wonderful to see all that at once. Travel the world and get paid.

Carnival in Peru. This owner decorated his truck.
Picture was taken close to the border.

Mountain view and life near Lake Titicaca

Machu Pitchu in Peru with my friends

Mountain view on miners' route to Tintaja

Plaza de Armas in Arequipa, Peru

Loading my motorcycle on the container ship. It was a very emotional and exciting moment.

The Captain and me off the coast of Ecuador

The Captain and me. This bread went into his freezer.

Two cooks and one waiter in the kitchen

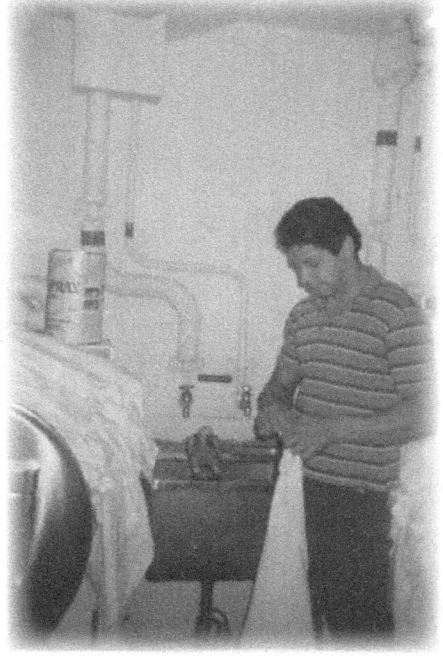

Albero, the laundry man, gets help
and supervision from Jaco

ECUADOR

March 8th we arrive in Ecuador's coast. In the morning comes a tugboat to guide us into the harbor. It is hot and very humid outside, an over cast. We don't stay long outside, inclusive the captain. We are close to the equator. We pass many small dreamful islands. It's so beautiful with palm trees, very green. You just want to stay. It is a long canal to Guayaquil. I was glued to the window watching this paradise. I chat with the boat pilot, and he tells me on Thursday a strong earthquake destroyed the pan American highway to Quito, the capital. There is a detour on a dirt road. My heart slides into my pocket from disappointment. I can't go to Quito, the devil is in charge. It is not meant for me going to Quito. I fell in a depression, as well I don't know how long the ship will be in the harbor. At one pm we arrive in the harbor, it is a different world. I am very disappointed. Jaco is happy in the laundry room. A broomstick goes from his cage to the sink, he is able to walk back and forth for exercise. Jaco always cheers me up. It's Sunday and with the electrician I go to the city. The locals are very dark and friendly. At the plaza we see a fire-eater showing off. We stroll the city. It was a fabulous day, however it was very humid and hot. With my companion it was no problem to get back onboard. The next day, the captain had company. A local assistant, we sit together talking. The local says to the captain, "Veronika is an adventurer and has no fear and nothing to loose." It is nice to travel the world by ship, I interrupt, is there a ship going to the Galapagos islands? Yes, there is. We ask for the price. Our hair stands up. Yes, the tourists have more money than the locals. That's why we ask for more, he continues charmingly. I have a house on Galapagos and in need of a cook. I shook my head, the captain defended me always with a smile. She doesn't want to be an employee. She is her own boss. Stubborn, unimpressed he continues talking. He needed a cook. I was not it. He tried to win and get his way. I live from the captains pocket and don't work. We looked at each other and smiled. We saw his bitterness. He couldn't get his cook. I leave the hopeless situation.

The next morning there is a German ship "The Trans Nave" in the harbor, from Bremen with a Panamanian flag. Captain Uribe encourages me to visit the Germans. They are friends to him. The German sailor are surprised to hear I travel on a containership. The transnave has ten German engineers and the rest of the crew is Panamanian. It is a huge ship, very clean and refrigerated. The German sailor take me on a tour chatting. The Germans charter their ships, since German laws are so strict. The German employees are to expensive. My dream to become a sailor is gone and I couldn't live with these ice cubes of people. He was polite and that's it. I went to see Jaco and Alberto doing laundry. He complains that Jaco eats to much. He brings him fresh apples, bananas, and corn pieces. I smile at him. Jaco likes your service and to be served from you. He is not impressed. Everybody loves snacks, right? Jaco. I got to know my way around the ship better, to the kitchen, storage, and the bridge. I stay away from most people to avoid accidents. I owe it to the captain. I still hear his voice, a few men will fall in love with you. Do what you have to do. My heart shouts "NO," I don't want to break any hearts and don't want to see tears when I leave in Panama. So I stay to myself. commuting only to the captains office, kitchen and bridge. I felt so free, so happy. The whole world is open. to me. I plan to travel the world for four to five years.

March 11th Captain Uribe congratulates me to my birthday. I bake fast a English teacake. The cooks have long been my friends. They comment on how fast and clean I work. They are middle aged, we talk, tell stories, and jokes. They always feed me well and I have treats for me. Everybody loved my birthday cake. The whole crew compliments my baking. Good taste, and not to sweet. Happy about their complements, I went to bed with a tie. I was honored.

March 13th we leave Guayaquil. I am happy, there was nothing to see or do. A boring time in the evening. I wake up in the morning and look out of the window and see the ocean and sun. Now I fell great again. My moral is high. When I feel lonely, I look for the cooks, the waiter or the officers. We always have fun. You have to make the best in life. Sometimes the quiet is nerve wrecking, so I go look for Jaco. I hear voices in the hallway and look around. Nobody, I follow the voices coming from the laundry room. I think Jaco must have company. I Peek around the corner and see Jaco happily sitting in his cage talking to himself. He cheered me up.

COLOMBIA

March 14th in the afternoon we arrive in Buena Ventura, Colombia. It is called the worst harbor in south America. The captain told me often, I was lucky to get on board in Lima. Here I would have had to wait a week or longer to get on a ship to cross the channel. I have to change cabins, to the third floor. It has less luxurious and smaller. The manager comes on board for inspection. He will occupy my cabin. In the evening I go with Martin on land. We walk around the city, its dirty, filthy and it rained all day. We pass lots of bars, girls waiting for customers. Caribbean music comes from every door. It invites to dream. We visit a disco and stay. A young tall black guy asks me to dance. We dance for hours, like a rack on a stick. He barely lets me rest for one or two songs. More sailors pour in, joining us. They look at me and the black dude. He hangs on me like a parasite. About two in the morning, Julio and I return to the ship tired and drunk. Sunday morning, I help in the kitchen. Pellito the cook has not found his way home. We make jokes about him. When he comes back, he has to wash himself with one kilo of soap to get clean and kill all the germs and illnesses he picked up in town. We miss Pelitos help today. We have more work. Lots of women are coming to visit their husbands. Everybody introduces their wife to me, I am glad I had no affair with them. I would have been not able to look their wife's in their eyes. We served barbeque, potatoes, and fruit salad. Martin sings the sailor song to the music. It is a happy, joyful reunion and gathering. Captain Uribe gets company, too. I retrieve to my cabin and dream.

Monday march 16th my dream to go to Cali is gone. A 500 meter dirt slide closed the road. I am unhappy. Tuesday march 17th the news comes the road is reopened. Mr. Colina the Taxi driver takes me to Cali and it is not very expensive. It is a very windy road, only taxis no buses drive there. The view along the green, tropical coast is terrific. We go up in the mountains, a very windy dangerous road and steep cliffs. I get Goosebumps just looking down. Lots of warning signs for sharp curves makes this a tense ride and drive. I kept my eyes on the road glad to be dizzy free. Later we stop at a view point to overlook the breath taking scenery and have a cup of good coffee. Mr. Colina squeezes me like a lemon with many stupid questions, I answered them bored. I wondered if these people ever read a book. It was a two hour drive. The city of Cali is on a plateau, surrounded by mountains. On top of one mountain is a Christ, on others are crosses. A young well dressed man on his way to work makes a detour guiding me to the exchange office and bank. I hope you are not late for work. He shrugs it off. I thank him several times. I walk along a river, looking at the city, there is nothing special to see. The air is sticky. Tired from walking I sit on a bench in a park. Watching peoples kids playing in the sand, and school kids pass by. The women are very elegantly dressed. It is very noticeable. It is a joy. Cali is known for that. Afterwards I visit a small museum. I was not impressed or lets say I have seen so many in my life. At 5:30 pm I wait in the city park for Vera, a sailor. Again watching the fashionable, elegantly dressed women. No one is dressed alike. At six pm Vera arrives, we greet and go to the cinema. He as well spent the afternoon looking for cheap hotels. The woman smiles one room? Yes, says Vera, with two beds I finished the sentence. The room had a bath inside, which is uncommon. We slept in separate beds. Vera has a girlfriend which I respect. He showed me pictures of her. We sleep in get up late in the morning. We get coffee served at the room. I get his coffee, Vera has to go with a empty stomach to the doctor. He has stomach cramps all the time. For hours we sit in the Doctors waiting room. I think, what a waste of time. At one pm its finally his turn. I wait impatiently for him. The result is a stomach ulcer. He gets a list of medicine and a diet plan. We rush to the taxi, it leaves only once a day for Buena Ventura. On the way we run into our companions they are in a hurry, too. The beautiful drive back lets me forget everything. In the evening is a party at the ship from the ship agency. Lots of new faces, some people even introduces themselves to me. Dorthe the captains wife acts as the hostess, running the whole show. No glass stayed empty and plenty of food is on the table. She sees everything She should be visiting only and relaxing. It is a nice evening, but I feel uncomfortable with all these strangers asking me questions.

  March 19th Dorothy is very popular, everybody wants to hang out with her. I can't wait to meet her, I have heard a lot about her. In the morning I go with Eliza to the post office and buy cassettes. The city is very dirty and smelly. At times we held our nose. I watch my pockets closely after all its a busy harbor town. I'm glad I didn't have to wait here for a ship. The black guy from the disco is again on my heels, I try to shake him off repeatedly. I tell him to leave me alone. I have no interest in you. We danced that night and that's it. He was disappointed. Elisa and I have lunch together and stroll casually back to the ship. In the afternoon I finally meet Dorothy alone. She is a tall good looking outgoing Person. She has blond hair, dark eyes always smiling. We talk in German for a while. Of course she likes to see Jaco, the famous parrot. She has an Amazon parrot at home. Jaco likes her, right away. He goes to her, like he knew her all his life. That surprised me and shy Albero the laundryman. That evening he invites me, we sit and drink a strong liquor I never had before, we had a good time. Everybody is happy to be home.

March 20th At one in the afternoon I teach the sailors wife, how to bake a English teacake and make bread. Ambitious they take notes of every step, every ingredient. I have the recipes in my head. They are astonished of how fast and quick I can work and how clean my workplace is. The cleanliness is important to avoid bugs, insects and anything else in this humid climate. I laugh about them and admit time is money. I have been Self employed for a long time, just staying above water. Eight loafs of whole wheat bread is for the captain. He is very happy, to be filling his freezer. We took a picture. The captain and me with the breads. We celebrate with a glass of wine. Everybody is happy, but I think to myself. I am quite heavy, jealously I look at the skinny wife's. They were all chatting, they enjoyed my short baking training. The days are passing, boring days, I wanted to travel to the interior of Colombia, but the ship could leave any day. How nice it is on the ship, there is a drawback, you are like a tied up dog. One evening the captain and his wife invited me for dinner, after a boring day. Astonished he asks? Nobody invites you? Nobody takes you out? No, I said. That is OK, thinking to myself I didn't want to get close to anyone. When its time to leave, no tears are falling. We went to a Hotel restaurant, very elegant we ate fish with champagne. I was exited to get to know Dorothy better. She is always nicely dressed and her hair combed back in a bird nest. A very attractive woman and well respected like her husband. They liked my outfit, skirt with matching blouse in pastel color with a wild designs from brazil with my hand made shoes from Korea. It was a very nice evening. I am excited to be soon in Panama to drive my bike again, but on the other hand very unhappy to leave the ship and my friends. One day the captain and his wife invited me for for lunch, ceviche with tomatoes and onions. A rational plate on the coast. We listen to older Colombian music. We sit on the window, in an older building overlooking the ocean, while a ocean breeze was blowing. I look down to the ocean we are high up, Goosebumps go down my spine. The garbage is floating in the ocean washing ashore, but palm trees surround all the shacks on high beams. I am sad how careless people are, but the food was good. The owner is very friendly. He knows Uribe for a long time and enjoys our interest in oldies. I turned my back to the ocean, to enjoy the good company and happiness. The restaurant is relative, big with several tables and a dance floor.

  The last evening in port, most sailors were gone. I decided to go to town alone. As always I dressed nice, a skirt with a blouse. I have to get out, the roof is falling on my head, I think frustrated, just to get out. On the entrance of the ship, I run into a few sailors, smiling they ask, where are you going? Casually I say to town. Alone, is the surprised answer! Yes, why not. A middle aged man in civilian clothes says kooky, I go to town as well. No, thank you, I go alone. It goes back and forth in our conversation. They are a huge doorstop I have to pass. All of a sudden I hear a motorcycle, my ears sharpen. You have a bike? Nosy I ask what kind. He smiles a Kawasaki 250 dirt bike. My eyes get bigger, it was always my dream to drive a dirt bike. I turn the conversation around. I go with you to town, under one condition. You let me drive your dirt bike. He laughs hard. Do you doubt I can drive a bike? He did. The sailors defended me and stand on my side. It made me feel good. Many men are selfish and macho. After a long discussion I ask for the key, he hands it to me. I turn on my heels and walk down the bridge. I see a yellow Kawasaki parked. I turn around. Is this your bike. The owner stands on the railing joking with the sailors officers. Look she wants to drive. I think his laughs will pass. I. ask him several times

I mean, let's go. He laughs about me, makes jokes about me. My patience was over, I sit on the bike, and figured out how to start the engine. He still stands on the railing talking and laughing. What a wash woman, men are a bigger talker than women. I think angry, they can talk forever. I give gas. Are you coming or not? I ask angry again. Now he comes fast, wanting me to get off the bike. I deny. Get behind me or I go alone. He educates me. Here drives the man, the woman sits in the back. Not today, I give gas again. He gives up and sits behind me. Proudly I drive through the harbor. Whistles come from every everywhere. I felt great. The uniformed guards saw us coming, they were laughing. You got a chauffeur today, we laughed with them. We drive into town. People line the streets, looking at us, shouting, whistling behind us everybody knows him. They found it amusing that a woman was driving. It felt like the circus came to town or the queen drives through. It feels so good. I opened the throttle and made pirouettes for them, the people got more exited, the voices got louder, my passenger shouted back to them. I haven't had so much fun in a long time. We drove criss cross through town no direction, no destination. After touring the whole town I asked him politely. Where do you want to go?

The people cheer, whistle. It is priceless. I'm having so much fun. He tells me to stop at a restaurant to have a beer. We walk in, people look at us, greet Amin the bike owner and businessman. It was a wonderful time to be with these people. So we drive around town from one bar to the next. I always drive, sometimes I mess up. I have a problem to find the neutral. He explains the gears. One up, second, third, fourth down. Nervous Amin asks for his key. No, I am driving and start the motor put in the gear. Fast he climbs behind me. He always gives me directions, this time out of town. I get nervous, what does he has on his mind? All a sudden he puts his arms around me. I have a bad feeling, I open the throttle, he let's go, but hangs on me like a monkey not to fall down. Then he tells me to make a right turn. It's dark there. I deny him, I know exactly what he has in mind. He makes two more attacks every time I open the throttle. He clinches on me like a monkey. He finally gave up. Thank god, I was relieved. At the first intersection I made a U-turn returning to the city. The road is divided with flower islands and fenced in to avoid people stepping on them. Back in town, we visited several more bars. We get invited several times to more beer. Amin you have a driver today, everybody laughs including us. One orders drinks, curious the men ask where are you from? We talk, laugh have a great time. With the last beer Armin asks harshly for his keys. You are drunk. With dry humor I respond, not more than you are. I smile and get up. I felt the alcohol held on the chairs and staggered out to the bike. At the harbor checkpoint, three young soldiers stand there smiling. I stop, I couldn't help to ask, you want to see my pass? With a big smile from ear to ear. All three laughed, waved us through, in good spirit and high emotions. I drive in circles around the harbor ground. Amin was nervous, I could feel his body shivering. He begs me to drive slower and watch out for for the train tracks. On purpose I took them in a sharp angle, he clammed on me. I did more tricks and had so much fun with him. I could feel his soaked body. I asked him casually? Are you afraid? I intensified the game and drove tighter circles, speed up, did slaloms, crossed more train tracks. Full of happiness, proud of myself to drive a dirt bike, while Amin started praying " ave maria"to the father in heaven. He saw his last hour coming.I enjoyed this. The macho shivering like a little duck. Our ship came in sight. I saw a group of sailors walking. As we came closer I recognized my companions. In the front row were the cooks, I circle around them. No one pays us any attention. I greet them with no answer, while Amin started to relax his grip on me. My companions must have a great night, they are deep in their conversations. They don't realize its us. I get angry, and make my circles smaller. Ready for my last attack I almost drive over the cook feet, while I lowered my head to look him in the eyes. He had his eyes on the ground, intensified speaking to his friend. I ask him Do you know me? His head went up laughing, greeting us. I continued driving circles around them, accompanying them all the way to the ship.I stopped at the ship. Amin got fast off the bike without wasting time. I laughed and he was dripping wet.I turned off the motor and gave him his keys. Happy, entertained, I thanked him for the evening. Drunk like a house, I could hardly stand straight, I staggered up the bridge holding on the railing, sometimes the feet wanted to give up under me. Halfway up my companions arrived. They were all happy, laughing, joking. Surrounding now Amin and chatting to him bored from listening I pulled myself up the bridge, while holding on the railing to keep my balance. On the ship the captain greeted me smiling with a few sailors. I told him briefly about my evening. They all laughed with me, happy and very drunk I went straight to my cabin. Loneliness overcame me. After a while I joined the happy sailors, everybody talking, waiting for the departure.

Dorthee, Capt. Uribe
We had dinner at a nice hotel in Buena Ventura

A view from a restaurant in Buena Ventura, Columbia
The Captain, Dorthee and I had ceviche there.

A view of Cali from a bridge

Rest stop on the way to Cali in the mountains
Vera and me

PANAMA

In the morning the captains calls me to see him in his office. Fast and excited I run upstairs. As always he has that special smile. Have a seat, he said pointing at the chair in front of him. I have to tell you something. This morning I spoke with panama's official, and told them proudly, that I have a German girl with a parrot on board traveling to America. Panama radioed back. The parrot must go 40 days in quarantine, it costs a dollar a day. To unload the motorcycle is 50 $ and to fumigate the bike is 50$, I almost fell out of my shoes. In shock I visualized Jaco sitting in a dirty cage, where no one can touch him. He may die there or I may never see him again. Jaco is a happy well loved clown. Devastated I got myself under control. I will tape his beak and tuck him under my shirt and put the coat over it and smuggle him through customs. The captain protested right away. No you don't. I took the responsibility to have you onboard of this ship. I thought about it, he is right. I owe him, how could I pay him back? I don't want Jaco to spend 40 days confined in a cage and I don't want to wait 40 days, sitting around here. A light went on. Mr. Uribe would you like to take Jaco home? He looks at me. You have to talk to my wife, she is the expert with parrots, animals are her expertise. I went to ask Dorothy and she said " yes" right away. No problem. Jaco could go home with her to Colombia. She has one and the neighbor has one. We fantasized about what Jaco will tell these Amazon parrots from his trip. We laughed. Jaco will be in good company. It was hard, but I gave Dorthy all the travel documents from Jaco and his pass until Mexico. It was all easier said then done. I excused myself and went to see Jaco to tell him all the news. He listened patiently agreeing with me. When I return from America I will pick you up in Colombia. For now you have a good home and you'll be in good hands. You will like Dorthy and there will be other parrots in their big green yard. Four more days in a cage then you will be in a big yard, with big trees. You are my best friend and very brave. I'm sorry that you had to live so long without green, surroundings. Please be good to Dorthy and behave. Jaco answered in his own voice. I felt a little lighter after talking to him, but my heart was heavy. I went to look for Albero, he wasn't in the kitchen. He ate breakfast in the mess hall alone. I greeted him and asked a few questions. Could you take care of Jaco for four days? Yes, he said astonished. Before he could ask me anything, I was out the door. He looked confused and wondered about me. I raced to my cabin to get my luggage, and took one last look around to make sure I didn't forget anything. The launch boat was here. It was time to say good bye to the captain and his wife. We shook hands and smiling he says. If Jaco doesn't see you, he won't feel the pain. That sentence I heard several times from him. I thanked the captain and his wife for everything with a forced smile, avoiding to cry It was very hard to continue traveling without Jaco, my best friend. He is everything to me,

    I was heartbroken. I continued thinking Jaco was in good hands, but my life is all of a sudden empty and without a purpose. I wished I had Jaco tucked under my shirt, smuggling him into the country, but I can't do that to the captain. Once more we looked each other in the eyes, Jaco will be fine, he said. The ship agent from Panama was ready to go, and I followed him. In the hallway I heard my name and I turn around to see my companions. I waved at everyone briefly with tears in my eyes and biting my tongue not to cry. I couldn't talk. I wanted to leave without tears, no broken hearts from the guys. Now I am the one with a broken heart. It was hard to leave the ship and my companions that I had gotten used to. I had a good time and a good caring captain. The bike got loaded on to the boat and we got on and took off. A few sailors stood on the railing waving and I waved back while fighting my tears. I couldn't talk or I would have a cried like a castle dog. Jaco staying back was the end off the world for me. The men on the boat just looked at me. They were small and well dressed. They could feel me and understood. We barely spoke. We arrived at the busy harbor and people were everywhere. They lifted the bike out the boat. One Panamanian got the bike and we followed him. The climate is hot and humid like a steam room. We were a mile from the sun. We got instructions to sanitize the bike. A few tears came down my cheek and I wiped them away. It is hard not to think about Jaco. The busy hustling workers just looked at me as they were sterilizing my bike. One friendly Panamanian explains. That everything from the south is from the jungle or forest and could possibly bring illnesses. I just shook my head about his attitude, do what you have to do, I said. How much do I owe you? Five US dollar. I paid him, then he sent me to immigration. All of the officers were very friendly and one tells me to follow him to his office. He stands behind his desk smiling like he had just won the jackpot. Now where is the parrot? I was not happy, grumpy and hurt I say" I don't have him and you don't get him. Repeatedly he asks for Jaco. I got more upset Jaco's loss was so painful. I just turned on my heels and walked out of his office, On the way out I ran into an agent and I stopped him to show the letter from Reynaldo. He doesn't know the address, but offers me to follow him to his air conditioned office to look it up on the map. Together we look it up on the city map. He prefers to speak in English and I didn't care, but I enjoyed the cool air. It is on the outskirts of the city, he explains. He was so polite, but I got more and more restless. My eyes were burning and I was fighting to keep from crying. I tried to be polite and said. It will be alright if I don't meet these people. For now I just want to continue on my trip and get out of the city. He realized that and was sympathetic with my pain. He offered me to guide me out of the city. He was driving his car and I followed him on my bike. It was a big wide freeway just like in America. I was blown away, just speechless. In the humidity it was hard to breath. I focused on driving, the road made a turn, he stopped and gave me the last instruction. We were at the outskirts now, I thanked him several times for his kindness and help. I was relieved to leave the big city behind. The freeway went now thru beautiful tropical scenes, passing sugar cane fields and a sugar factory. My heart felt lighter and I sang a song to put the loss of Jaco on the side. Driving for hours in the burning sun with high humidity became a challenge. It was a dreamful fascinating drive. Passing mountains, grazing cows and very few trees and passing small villages. It was a wonderful feeling. I Stopped to fill up my tank and surprisingly they took Us dollars, everybody seems laid back and friendly. Many passing cars waved at me. I was surprised. Do I look American? Is it my T-shirt and less luggage I wondered. In the afternoon a shower passes through. At a gas station with a store in nowhere I stop to buy crackers and juice, as I came out the door I thought Bud Spencer was approaching me. He looked just like him with his cowboy hat and cowboy outfit. I stared at him as he passed me. Am I in America or Panama? I wondered for a second. I ate and felt better continuing on the good pan American highway until the city of Santiago. It's afternoon and I look for a motel, to my disappointment all the rooms are upstairs. Frustrated and bitter I asked two tall young men for a motel. I have been looking for a while. One my age offers to stay at his big house for the night. Skeptical I follow him. A big nice German shepherd dog greets us at he gate. This is Valentine. We are instantly friends, two Germans. He loves to be patted. I think of Jaco. I wonder how is he doing? I agreed to stay the night. We left the bike in the yard. We chat and all of a sudden Valentine jumps the four foot tall fence and runs away. Andre bolts behind him. He is going to see his girlfriend I shouted behind him. A few minutes later a young girl comes to visit. Well that must be Andre's girlfriend. I told her Andre is chasing his dog. We went inside and talked a little and I asked her. What should we do. The kitchen looked like a single mans kitchen. To change my thoughts I suggested to her lets clean the kitchen and then the house. We worked hand in hand and time passed quickly. Andre came back with his dog and looked around astonished. We explained we had nothing to do and I sat all day. He offers me to stay for a while. I deny and ask him about his wife. With great sorrow he tells me his life story. It's been two months since he has been divorced and lives alone. His ex-wife and child lives in Panama city. He got married very young. They argued a lot about daily life and money. I like Andre and Valentine very much, both are very sympathetic, but I have to continue on my trip. Later he brought dinner. We had Chicken, potatoes and pineapple juice. It tasted very good. His friends came over and they started drinking, smoking marijuana and light conversation. I go to bed, Andre had an extra mattress and put it on the floor for me. At night we ran into each other on the way to the bathroom. He excuses himself for the noise with his friends. I tell him it's alright it is your home. Enjoy your life and every lucky moment. No one knows how long it will last. I think of Jaco. One of his friends begs me to stay longer, we could take the day off and go to the river. I thank him it is well meant, but I wanted to continue on my trip to avoid a relationship.

America: Final Destination

The next morning I got up early, Andre is disappointed that I wouldn't stay. I explained to him that I have to continue to America and return to Jaco. It was hard to say, goodbye. When you return, there is a open house for you, said Andre. I thanked him for everything. I got on my bike and take off. Singing a song, on the road again. Watching with one eye on the rising sun and dreaming into the day. The flat scenery changes to mountains, passing coffee plantations and palm trees. The fresh cool air keeps me awake.I love nature and listening to my bike motor makes me feel so free. People greeted me, but one thing is missing. Panama jack in his typical tropical clothes and hat. I see two boys sitting along the road with a nice mountain of high stack grapefruits. I had to stop and buy some. They were 25 cents each. The green mountains are so wonderful with a fresh breeze going. I push forward, at ten o'clock I arrive at the border faster than I had thought. I left Panama to go through a neutral zone to Costa Rica, but the border is closed from eleven am until one pm.

COSTA RICA

Angry and upset I ask a man, why is it closed it is only ten o'clock? Costa Rica is one hour ahead, he was waiting,too. I feel stars falling off my eyes, why did I hurry? To wait two hours on the border? Angry I pass the street vendors selling jewelry and clothing from Panama, Ecuador. Colombia's embroidery is very similar. It was a long impatient wait. Before one we all stand in line waiting for immigration to open. They took their time, smiling he sends me to customs. You need to purchase a bike insurance otherwise you can't enter. Sixteen dollars for insurance I was in shock, but had no choice. Another officer asks me smiling" where are you going? Costa Rica patiently he says, San Jose. I look at him confused and get my letters out of my suitcase. I showed him the address and he gives me directions. I was numb, my heart hurt. I left relieved, enjoying the tropical green scenery again. It was may be ten minutes into the country when a rainstorm surprised me. It rained so hard I could hardly see my front tire and the road. I drove blind while slowing down. Luckily it didn't lasted long and the rain eased, but still it was pouring in buckets. Frustrated I looked for a house or a shed, nothing not even a tree. I got soaked to the skin and the temperature dropped, too. Then my engine quit and I got upset. It seems everything is going wrong. What can I do? No people, nothing around to get help. Well I think in humor, if you love your bike you push it. I started walking with water filled squeaking boots. A couple of cars passed me, they wouldn't stop I kept on walking. Thank god the rain stopped and not long after I heard a motorcycle coming. Happily, I turn around with my thumb up hoping he would stop and help. He did. Excited I tell him my pitfalls. Probably the sparkplug got wet, he said. It just won't start. How far is a village? Not to far. I talked him into towing me. After a few attempts it worked. He knew a mechanic. Surprised faces stared at us as we pulled in his building. He doesn't see that everyday. Friendly, laid back he thoroughly inspected the bike. We talk, but honestly I understood only half of what he said. It took a while to solve the problem. They were curious about where I was from, I told them about my journey, shivering while a constant breeze came through. All were astonished and impressed. It took a good hour to fix my bike I asked him how much? Nothing, it surprised me. I thanked him several times and asked him for direction leaving the town. The green country was so impressive. Its mountains, agriculture and isolated little forests made it an idyllic picture. A dream. A curvy bad road brings me back to reality. I had to shift gears constantly. To my luck came another rainstorm drenching me to the bone. There was nothing dry on me, but I continued driving passing trucks as they soaked me even more. That's why it is so green, I said. When it finally stopped raining my rear tire felt funny. I pull over and realized I had a flat tire in the middle of nowhere. My patients are over, I said to myself. Today everything is going wrong. In bad humor I get off my bike and push it again in the mountains. Every time I hear a car coming I would hold my thumb out, but nobody stops. So I continue walking and later I got lucky and a small pickup stopped. A young couple got out, I showed them my flat tire and asked if they could give me a lift to the next town. Surprisingly they didn't mind. Their back was loaded with crafts and baskets. The small skinny woman made room and we loaded the bike. They didn't talk much, but I was happy about their help. She was driving and her tall skinny husband sat in the middle like the rooster. We talk a little, I could see who is wearing the pants in this relationship. The man is very sympathetic. They invite me for dinner, yucca with meat at a eatery. Where is the salad or the vegetables I think to myself. They asked me if I would like to drive with them to San Isidro a bigger town. It would be easier to find a mechanic there. I agreed. I was cold from my wet clothes. Then in middle of nowhere there was a checkpoint. We stop and he inspects the back, officially he asks, Why is there a bike in the back? Quick I explain, I have a flat tire and these nice people are taking me to a mechanic The officer became friendly and let us go. We drove higher into the mountains, the couple asked if I would like to stay at their reserved motel. Yes I would. We arrived there before dawn. The owner in a snow white apron came running to greet the couple. They asked if she has an extra room. She did. They've known each other for a long time. Happy, caring she shows me a nice room with white linen. It felt like Germany. I looked forward to a hot shower and dry clothes. I opened my suitcase to get out dry clothes and to my horror all were damp. Well at least I will get a hot shower and crawl into bed. That was my thought, but the water was cold. I took a cold shower, put my half wet clothes on and crawled in a the damp bed. I couldn't get warm after a while I got up and walked in the street trying to find a warm place. Without luck I returned. It was a long cold night.

March 28th early in the morning I went to a mechanic with a freezing body. Watching him fix my flat and some minor maintenance. Happy, I returned to the motel good and loaded my bike. Clumsy, I turn and my bike crashed on the ground. My helmet was on the handlebar and the visor was broken. I was angry. I brought the bike to a stand now I see something dangling. What is this I thought? I took a closer look and it was the clutch, I felt helpless. One thing after another, because my head is somewhere else, at Jaco.

I returned to the mechanic and kindly he goes with me to the Honda dealer. Everybody in this country is so polite and friendly I am not used to that. He looked at me and said, sorry we don't have your model here and no parts for it. Frustrated I ask do you have something similar? I can't drive without it. Friendly he looked and found a used one. It was much bigger, but it fit and I was very happy and touched by their friendliness and kindness. In town I see the couple again selling crafts. They offer me to go together this afternoon to San Jose. I thanked them for the offer. You found food? They said Yes, I reply. I was drinking cold milk and eating crackers and I am looking for the sun to get warm. They wave. Driving up the mountain the air is fresh, many BMWs and Mercedes pass me. That means people have money. In the sun it is warm and it felt good drying my clothes. At 3 400 m is a police official. The policeman said, I am brave to travel alone. I thanked him for the compliment. The scenery is so beautiful I dream into the day. The city of San Jose is in a valley. In a suburb I filled my tank at a Texaco station. A big bully looks mean at me. A brother from Bud Spencer I think with humor. I gave him a grapefruit and walk away to pay.

Curious he looks at my license plate. I can read in his eyes, where is Villarrica. I drove to the beginning of he city, lost I asked a young man in a jeep for direction. What's the address. I dig out my letter from

Reinaldo. He laughs it is not here. Confused and careless I look at him. Jaco's loss was painful. He sits there thinking there is a new road opening today through the national park Browly. That road is much shorter to that address. I was relieved to hear that, avoiding the city traffic. Kindly he guided me to the entrance and wished me a good trip, I thanked him, People were lining the roads, it felt like a parade. The weather was beautiful, only blue skies and sunshine. There were Red Cross booths, first aid booths mixed in with food booths. I always saw them to late or better said I was going to fast downhill. My stomach was crumpling and desired some food and the booths were gone. The park was gorgeous, high mountains, green valleys, bird singing just stunning. A concern overcame me how this park will be in harmony with traffic coming through and killing animals crossing the road? The advantage is that everybody can see the park from their car, without putting a foot on it. In the valley came the exit for Rio Frio. At the first country store I stop to ask for directions, but nobody knew the village. Now I realize how hot it is. I had a raincoat on under my leather coat to keep the cold wind out. One pickup driver knew the village. Follow me, he said. I didn't get a chance to take my coat off. He drove so fast, like a slaughtered pig through the banana plantations. I had a hard time keeping up with him, while sweating like a monkey in my sauna rain suit. Luckily he slowed down until he saw me and took off again. At times I thought I would get a heatstroke. I couldn't enjoy the scenery of small farms, the crossing of several weathered bridges sometimes I preferred to cross the river instead, afraid the bridge would collapse. Just trying to keep up. In a small village he was waiting for me, stating that is it. I thanked him. I looked at a few scattered homes and asked for the family. Nobody knew I thought that was strange. Someone read my body language and came forward stating to know the family. I was relieved. It is tricky to find, but how do you explain it? Go back and after the fourth bridge in a curve turn left. It is the third house on the left. Happy again I got on my bike counting the wooden bridges with deferred maintenance. Sometimes I crossed the river instead. Not paying attention I had to do the route twice to find the left turn all on gravel road. Then there came another bridge, partly broken. It looked scary, carefully I cross it in zig sag fashion. It's cracks suspicious, I prayed it wouldn't break.

America: Final Destination

If it cracks again, my heart will stop, finally I made it to the house. A simple wooden house on posts half a meter of the ground with a porch. What a dream home. That's not what I expected, Reinaldo told me they lived in the city. I clap in my hands, since there is no doorbell, a young boy appears. Surprised he looks at me and I ask him, politely is this family Villalobos? Yes, the mom shows up. I give her the letter and a gift from Reinaldo, while I was still in shock and what I was told and what I see. However I was relieved to get rid of it. They were as surprised as me. She invites me into the house and to unload my bike. I did it with mixed feelings. These are very poor people and I came to burden them. It is very hot and humid. Every move you make is an effort and hard to breath. She offers me food, embarrassed I except it, I was starving. Thinking sadly I passed up all the hot dog stands. The food was very good. We were all uneasy of my visit, the boys talked to me, to got to know the stranger with a gift. While sitting on the porch on the floor overlooking the green scenery. I thought to myself how beautiful. Later I needed to use the bathroom. He guided me through the kitchen, I looked around it was filthy, my stomach almost turned. The outhouse was behind the house surrounded with a few Coconut trees. Really idyllic, I heard a noise looking around and see a parrot high up. The boy showed me proudly their pet parrot. My heart was delighted, a green Amazon with purple on the forehead. On the other hand it reminded me of Jaco, very painful. I put a smile on. My stomach started to hurt and I felt funny, but couldn't use the bathroom. We spent the afternoon at the porch while my stomach cramps worsened. She offered to take me to the clinic, I refused instead had some medicine, it gave me relief. The next morning my condition got worse and I have pimples on my stomach, my hands and eyes were swollen. With the whole family we drove by bus to the nearest by hospital in Rio Frio. It was packed. I was scared not having health insurance, but the doctor was cool. He explained to me that most people don't have insurance either, they pay a small fee. He gave me six shots, which made me feel sicker. I was ready to throw up. Friendly he explains that this is normal. It will go away and he wanted me to be hospitalized. I refused it's only a stomachache, I said. We had to promise to come back tomorrow if it worsens. He was so kind and friendly just wanting to help. I thanked him with a forced smile and returned to their home. I was the attraction as neighbors came to visit us we visit them. Down the street lived an old woman in a small house with a palm tree roof. They have very basic furniture and cooking for an old man laying on a stretcher high of the ground. These people are really poor. Glad we left. From here we crossed the river on a 4x4 to visit a family with four kids. She had a bigger house and was more modern. It was very pleasant, if I just would feel better. In the morning I have more pimples and show it to Rita Juan's wife. She is very concerned with the whole family we walk to the clinic Horqueta to get more injections and buy aspirin in the pharmacy. Eric the owner invites me to his house, everybody likes my blue eyes, I just laugh and leave. In the afternoon Juan her husband arrived with a friend. Albero a very outgoing friendly man. He speaks some English, we have a lot of fun talking and laughing. I was trying to hide my worsening condition, but they picked it up. We agreed in the morning we would take you with us to San Jose. My night was very bad, the strong pain wouldn't let me be comfortable in any position. Tossing and turning most of the night. Finally I heard voices early in the morning, relieved I got dressed, but my pants zipper wouldn't close and my shoes barely fit. My whole body felt swollen. I made my bed and see ants under my mattress a ice cold shiver goes down my spine. The doc said the pimples are ant bites. I waited on the porch under moonlight, it was so quiet and peaceful. Juan and his friend Albero came and I thanked his wife for everything. We drove in his Jeep on the bumpy road and stopped on the way at the local hospital in Rio Frio. The doctor recognized me right away. Concerned he took me in a room gave me six shot. She can't go back to the house her life is in danger, I don't have a bed available Don't worry doc, Juan said interrupting him. We are going to a hospital in San Jose. Doc was very relieved. I thanked him again for caring so much. At dusk we arrived in the city. First we stopped at his sisters house. They live in a quiet hood. She is a small, skinny with short black hair and very likeable. We regrouped as she served us coffee and then we drove to the general hospital. They turned us down. You have to go to a special clinic. We were all upset. So we drove to the hospital Mexico. A huge complex. At the admission, they asked many question, Juan handled most of them. He was always in good humor. In good spirit he pulled me aside. You need a health insurance provider in order to get admitted. My heart sunk in my shoes, I don't have one. Juan told them. You are an employee of our company. What a glorious idea. Remember if they ask you. You work for us. We do that because you got sick in our home. I was speechless and touched by there caring. I couldn't thank him enough. After a long wait a nurse came to put me in a room, and handed me a night gown. I overheard her saying to another nurse. Looks like food poising. I had to use the bathroom and passed a big mirror. I looked in there and could hardly recognize myself. I look like a big black market woman, with my face and lips so swollen. The only thing missing was the cigar. Preferably hanging at the corner of my mouth, to complete the picture.

  The nurse put me in a wheelchair. Juan and his friend left. I sat for hours in a cold hallway waiting to be seen by a doctor. Several times I asked a passing nurse for painkillers. They always say. The doctor will be right with you. Five hours later and different doctors were doing tests on me. A skin sample went to the lab. How long will it take to get the results? You will be here for three or four days. I felt like a guinea pig, he laughed. We are specialist and haven't seen this before. We are trying to find the cause and symptoms. I was alright with that. It was a big modern Hospital. I was glad to be here and get the medical attention. My pimples disappeared and I slept a lot. In the evenings Nelly, her sister Sereneida and their friend Elieth came to visit, I was so touched for their caring. They all live together and took turns visiting me.

    On the fourth day I was ready to leave the hospital, but the doctor denied it. I was all rested and bored now. Laying all day in bed, no radio and nothing to do. Next to me lays an older woman, astonishingly calm and peaceful. She has an intelligent son. We talked for a long time breaking the boring routine. Three times a day a good humored nurse gives me an injection. In the morning and evening comes another nurse with pills. Late mornings comes a group of doctors discussing each patients condition. This was our daily life. In the evening we got visitors, usually two girls came to check on me. Do you need anything? Yes I would love to have fresh apples. I wasn't allowed fruits. The hospital food was very bland. They brought me an apple sometimes two. I hid them in the drawer and ate them at night. When I couldn't sleep at night I walked up and down the hallway. I ran into a nurse, she sat with a teenage girl in a wheelchair. She was crying and moaning of pain, realizing she is the one from next door. We hear her all the time. What is the matter with her? Kindly the nurse says, she can't walk and has an incurable disease. She is in and out of the hospital, because of her father. He wants her home to rape her on a regular basis. I was shocked. She pleads to stay in the hospital or end her life. I no longer I felt annoyed by her crying. We prayed for her. That somehow her health and wellbeing improves and have her own life, away from her abusive father.

We got a new woman to our room. Middle aged, curvy. Very humorous, she often tells jokes. Her name is Negra, she is dark not black. We laugh a lot about her. She becomes our entertainer. I was scheduled for a stomach image from midnight until one pm that day no food, no water. it was a long wait. With burning thirst the doc instructed me to swallow a thick hose, I gagged a few times, but I couldn't swallow it. He got mad. I told to him cancel the test, I'll just live with stomach pains. Could I have some water now? At my room I drank one liter of water, my body rejected food. Often I asked the doctors when can I leave this windy, drafty hospital? On the sixth floor. With windows you can't open. I knew why? Seven people inclusive me thought about suicide to escape pain. They never answered. One nurse always joked with me, here comes your injection. Quickly I respond, I am not here. We all laugh, my body is here, my mind isn't. I show my behind, full of injections holes, it looks like a pincushion. Let's try the other side she says laughing. On Sunday evening after dinner I didn't feel to good, my joints ached. At night I woke up, and needed to use the bathroom and to my horror, I couldn't move from the neck down. Strong pain kept me awake. From time to time I looked over to the woman next to me, hoping she wakes up. She did after a while. Could you please ring for the nurse I can't move and I need to use the bathroom. She did, an advanced pregnant doc showed up. I explained it all, rudely she says I don't want to loose my baby for helping you to use the bathroom. I was shocked. It is normal after one allergy follows a second one. The pain is rheumatoid fever in the joints. That didn't sound very promising. The pain was almost unbearable. After an injection I felt better, but couldn't move. For three days I was paralyzed, the humorous nurses had to do everything for me. It was very embarrassing, but they had no choice. They feed me, gave me bedpans, and every morning put me in a wheelchair and bathed me. Everyday I improved, feeling came back to my arms, but the feet didn't belong to me. A couple of times I tried to get into the wheelchair, but ended up on the floor. The nurses scolded me, why didn't you wait? I needed to use the bathroom, I feel embarrassed to get helped all the time. Little by little, day by day my feeling came back. I had to learn to walk again. I was so grateful to walk a few steps. What a wonderful feeling to being able to walk.

  Friday morning a new doctor comes to our room. I beg him, let me leave the hospital. He looks through my files and says the blood work doesn't look good. You need your daily injection. I told him convincing my friends live a five minutes walk from the hospital. I can walk there to get my shots. He didn't like it. I continued talking the longer I stay here the sicker I get. Now I have internal hemorrhoids on top of everything else from lying in bed so long. I promise to go everyday to the hospital. Finally he gave in, this afternoon you can go home, he said. You need to call someone to pick you up? I did, full of joy and happiness I called. Elith came to pick me up at 3:30 in the afternoon. We hastily rushed to the door, we heard a voice. Stop you need to fill out the release form of the hospital. A big stack of papers and confirming my health insurance. My ten day hospital stay was over 10 000$ I almost fell out of my shoes. Finally we go to the office to meet co workers, and friends. Everybody was so friendly and kind. I was deeply touched of their generosity and caring. How they took on a total stranger. We got along so well immediately, like we knew each other for years. I had to promise to come back, since it got late.

Saturday morning we drive to the hospital. The security guard refuses my entry I explain to him I need to pick up my medicine. I showed him all my paperwork, then he let me go. On the way out I showed him everything. At noon I drive with Albero to the bus terminal to take the bus to Horqueta, to Sarripiel to visit his family and neighbors to Juan and Rita in the country. Albero is a very humorous man continuously he asks about my hemorrhoids. How will you sit in the bus with it? Humorously I respond. I will sit for a while on one cheek than on the other cheek. The bus takes the new route through the national park. It is cloudy and rainy. I take the trip better than expected. Albero warns me the bus only goes to Rio Frio from there we have to walk. I laugh, well then we walk. You with your hemorrhoids? He responds laughing. What choice do we have? I wondered. We reach Rio Frio at darkness. We get off the bus and he walks across a big parking lot. I followed him. He had his motorcycle stored. A 125 dirt bike, I was surprised and happy. Do you think it will hold two fat ones? I laugh, one cheeseburger and one double deluxe. In emergency I drive and you run behind me, we both laugh. Albero starts the engine and I sit behind him. The tire is half flat, he turns out to be an excellent driver on the dirt road. Slowly he goes around all the holes. My hemorrhoids are very grateful for that. His wife greets us very kindly with anticipation. They live in a small simple house. She shows me a bedroom. For the guest only the best. We sit together sharing the news. She heard from Rita that I got sick and took good care of me. Again I was touched of her caring. Often she asked is everything alright? Yes, thank you for your concerns. I hope you sleep well and leaves the room. It was quite a climate change from the cool mountain to the hot humid sticky climate. I crawled under the mosquito net and they sang all night into my ears. My skin itched like I fell in an anthill. In the morning she asked about my night, did you sleep well? At breakfast she shared the news. That under my mattress was an army of ants. I almost fell of the chair. There shows up Rita just to hear the news and we all laugh. I needed more clothes, so we all go to her home and socialize there. Around eleven we hear a bike driving up, clapping. An uncle came to visit. He introduces himself to me. We all sit together talking. He is well dressed and spoken. He proudly shows us his new motorcycle. A Java 350, I was impressed. Would you like to drive with me to San Jose? Yes, I would love too. I was excited, it beats taking the bus, we laughed. I grabbed some clothes and we left. He drove very careful. My bottom appreciated it. The scenery is so beautiful. Ranches, banana plantations, etc We drove along a river lined with big trees, so idyllic. He points at a cable with a hanging box. This is to cross the river. Would you like to get on it? Not today, but I would a loved to get on it. Since every step was painful. I was afraid I could not get up. We stare at the river for a while. I did with a broken heart for the lost adventure. He continued driving slowly and with passion explaining the sights. He is different I could feel something is on his chest. He became more and more sympathetic to me. We stop for lunch. We had a sandwich and a beer, at a newer part of town. He defiantly knows the area. Slowly the shy timid man starts talking. I do enjoy his company. He is happy not to be alone and I am glad not to sit in a bus. I really appreciate the drive, I said. The wind blows on our ears with blue sky, sunshine and not to warm. He is a gentleman always concerned about me. We both love to travel. We visit a new settlement of farmers and his friends. They burned the rainforest to plant mostly pineapples, plant some vegetables for themselves. The government hands out loans for the land, then the prices on pineapple dropped. They nearly lost their land, but with hard labor they saved it. It was disheartening to hear, but they managed to hold on. We were happy for them. We sit in front of their tiny one room home. It sleeps eleven people They spent all day outside. Proudly they show us their property, months of hard labor. The people are so friendly, hostile happy with their life. I asked for the bathroom which is away from the home. I walk slowly, stopping to overlook their property. Every step hurts, they must have thought I shit in my pants, the way I walked. I looked in their faces, they were involved in their conversation and didn't pay attention to me. Good, I was relieved. I love these people. They are poor, but make the best in life. They are so happy and content. We continue driving and stop from time to time and have a beer. It helped to loosen his tongue. He tells me his life story and he is deeply unhappy. I understand him very well. He traveled the world in the service and now he is misunderstood. He's a misfit in this society. Even his wife doesn't understands him. That's why he drives alone. I like him, we have fabulous conversations for two travelers. On an intersection in the middle of nowhere he asks if I am in a hurry to get to San Jose? No, I have time. Then we take the longer old scenic route. That sounded good to me. Life is worth living, despite the pain. Always put a forced smile on it. We pass coffee plantations in the mountains. He knew all the scenic stops and I wanted to see them all. We stop at a German fruit jam factory. Only the store was open since it was Sunday. During the week you can see the production. I was happy to see it. I bought two jars of jam. One for the Stevens. For a moment I thought I was in Bavaria, Germany or Switzerland. The scenery, the houses are so similar. It blew my mind. What a beautiful, wonderful day. I couldn't thank him enough. It was late afternoon we are still on the road and its getting chilly. It was already dark, when we arrived at Nelly's house. Surprised she welcomed us, with her two sisters we sat around the table and talk about our daytrip. I could feel a coldness between them and the uncle. Nelly looks with big eyes at me, saying: Veronika you with your bad hemorrhoids? I smile painfully. Yes they are still there. How could you drive all day through the country? Nelly continues wondering. I had to laugh about her. Today I had the opportunity of a life time, with an excellent guide and driver to see the country. I couldn't resist. Silently everyone starred at me. From now on they talked about family issues. There was a lot of tension and uneasiness. After he left Nelly told me his wife is very jealous and they don't care much for him. He is different. I agreed and do understand him. I have the same interest like him. I wasn't popular that night and went to bed. Easter week I spent mostly in bed. Twice a day I walked to the hospital for my injections, I promised Nelly to do it. That five minute walk took me almost half an hour due to pain. I slept a lot, listened to the radio for distraction. Often I woke up and didn't knew what day it was or if its day or night or I didn't knew where I was. When everyone was at work I showered. The enjoyable shower became torture to me. The soft water felt like needles on my body. I cried from pain. The same using the bathroom. After a few days I put all injections and pills aside. I'll just let the body heal itself. Eighteen pills and three injections a day is to much. It took a couple of weeks to get over the cruciating pain. It drove me almost insane and I had suicide thoughts. I was thinking of my parents, Nelly and her family, I can't leave a mess behind and prayed to get well every day. The house is like a hotel, Juan brings friends or guest come over for a few days or a week. Then there are gone for a while. It is a midsize house, a girls room, boys room and a couple guestrooms with basic furniture. Nelly is a good cook and I love her soups. I started to feel better and ventured out. I called Ray in California, he was concerned and wondered. Where are you? We haven't heard from you in a month. I was sick and in the hospital. When are you coming? I don't know, I said. Now my body is like a newspaper with daily new pains or aches. We laughed, keep in touch. Say hey to Nancy.

    On a Saturday Nelly and her boyfriend Frank bring me to the terminal. I take the bus to Horqueta to get my motorcycle I was getting better. They will follow tomorrow with their bike. The weather was cloudy and rainy through the park. Rita picked me up. Everyone is concerned about my health. They have me stay the night with Albero's family. We had a wonderful evening, talking and watching some TV until late. The next morning Nelly and Frank show up. We walk with the whole family and neighbors to the river to bath and swim. I was hesitant, I didn't have a swimsuit so I went in my underwear. Nobody cared. Everybody got in, it was a lot of fun. I found a log to lean on in the water, while watching everyone played or swam. The water was very cold, blue green. We stayed for a long time. When we got out of the water I realized the swelling went down. I was able to walk better. Cold and exhausted we walked back and changed into dry clothes and were ready for lunch. They were a noisy happy crowd. They tell me to find a friend and stay here. It was very tempting, but I am on a mission. My friends are waiting for me in California. Everybody is kind and friendly, begging me to stay. My plan is to go for one year to America and work and save money and buy a pick up truck. I'll return to Paraguay this coming year. I will visit all my good friends inclusive the parrot. Frank has a 125 Honda as well, but a different model. What an irony. His is blue and all steel. Mine is red with a lot of plastic. Frank got stuck a few times on the dirt road, I waited on them. On the way through the park we got rained on. I was a better and faster driver then him. How embarrassing for Frank. We always needled each other and joked.

Monday morning I went to see the dentist again. Here they call me by my middle name" charlotte."they liked that better. My friend doctor Sanchez Chien recommends that I stay here. Don't leave the country, he said. He was sincere. He gave me medicine for my ear infection and broke the news. You have an infected tooth. He treats the nerve. Only one tooth per visit, because many people are waiting. I thanked him. The people are so friendly. From here I visited the national museum to kill the time. I spent to much time in bed. My friends are doubting I continue my trip to America. jokingly I tell them. My body is like a newspaper with daily news. It seems everyday is something else wrong or hurting. I needed distraction. At the museum I met a group of English speaking students. In may they will fly to Washington D.C. We talked for a while, my English wasn't very good. Travel fever over came me. How many countries do I have to pass until America?

April 24th I get up very early, no one noticed it. I drove to the dental clinic, asking the chief dentist, if he could treat my teeth faster that I could continue on my trip. He denied. The nerve treatment takes time. I was disappointed. I felt like a burden to Nelly and her family. They always denied it. I got my humor back and they enjoyed my company. Every night they asked me where have you been? I always had a story to tell. We all laughed. My blue eyes caused the attraction. The next day I had to see the dentist again and Nelly invited me to her office. She works at the nurse section. Her coworkers surround me. They have heard a lot about me. Nelly introduces me to her boss. We talk for a long time. About politics and life. The guerillas are the problem in this country. Costa Rica is a poor country and has several international credits to pay. That's why the taxes are so high. The retirees get a pension and the unemployed financial help. Many Nicaraguans, Honduras and Guatemalan come hungry here to seek help.

America: Final Destination

Just like me, I finished the sentence. We all laugh. The Nicaraguan take the work from the ticaners away. This is missing. The guerillas get help from Russia with tanks and weapons from USA. He advises me sincerely to take the banana boat to America. Nicaragua is dangerous, he said. They have grenades hidden on the street. You Don't see them until you drive over, they explode. Everything flies in the air. He is afraid for me, that I die. Relaxed and calm I answer. I appreciate his concerns for me, but I am going through Nicaragua. If I hit a grenade I will die happy, with the thought. I at least tried. Again he advises me, not to go. I tell him firmly you sound like the consul in Paraguay. You take the highlight out of my trip. By not going through Nicaragua. He is shaking his head, and wishes me a safe trip. One last advice. Drive behind a truck. That is safer. I promised to do that.

On Saturday we are invited to an uncles sons wedding. Both in their early twenties, very sympathetic. Both are woodworkers and cabinetmakers. We attend the catholic church service. Take pictures and everybody is given a wedding favor. They had a small handmade crochet hat with two rings and their names on it. I find it cute. Afterwards we go to the community hall, it is a beautiful warm day, sunny and blue sky and Music is playing, we get a coke with liquor, and chicken with rice. Everybody is happy, laughing and dancing. We were having a wonderful time. Later we go to their home with only the family members for coffee and cake. The parents live in a small house. Give the newly weds one room, until they can afford their own house. I was touched by their kindness and how they help each other. This is paradise in Costa Rica. Family members ask me when do you continue? Never?? These people stole my heart I love them.

Sunday morning around ten o'clock Nelly and I drive on my bike to an inactive volcano in a national park.

Health wise I was doing better. The lust of adventure is overcoming me. I want to see more of the country and land instead of hospitals. I know of seven hospitals as patients and countless doctors. What an impression of Costa Rica. We laugh together. I think about captain Uribe. He loves Costa Rica, I had to promise to stay at least four weeks. I am here, but haven't seen much. The passage is in a small national park with a museum. We parked the bike and continue on foot to the volcano. We look inside a blown volcano. I see a variety of earth tones, with clouds are coming out. The museum was interesting, showing the history of the volcano. The whole country used to be a forest. Now it is may be 20% left. What a shame, some progress. On a picture it reads, When will be the last tree cut? Wow, what a foresight these people have. The population dates back to European settlers. Their skin is light, black hair and dark eyes. They have no military, only national guardsmen. We drive through lovely country and stop to see an English speaking friend from France and an aunt in Aulajelo. She was a very nice person. We had a wonderful day. Nelly and I visited aunt Lydia and as usual they invite us to eat. The poor always share their food. She crochet a tablecloth. We walked to the market with handcrafts. I bought a wall plate of Costa Rica for my parents, and a keychain sandal for Monika in Paraguay. A keychain house for Nelly and her housemates. As a souvenir so they won't keep losing their keys so easily. We returned to the house as the newly weds arrive. She is a down to earth person as well her husband. No make up or make believe. I like her a lot.

Tuesday April 28th we visited the hospital Mexico to pick up my results. Bad news. I have Colagenosis. They ordered a new test. Many people know me here, we have fun talking and joking around. I would love to stay here, I have so many friends. If Ray and Nancy Stevens wouldn't wait for me, I would stay. I told Nelly, Sereneida, Elith next week I continue my trip. They all start laughing. They heard me saying it several times. I put my trip off, because off another doctors appointment. I'll never leave here. My body is like a newspaper, daily news. I miss Jaco a lot.

Wednesday April 29th I wrote postcards and mailed a birthday card for my mom and the plate as a gift. And I gave a keychain sandal to Monika. She loves to wear sandals now she will have a second pair. When I am alone, I think depressed about Jaco. Without him my life is empty and unimportant. I shake it off. I visited a mechanic to get my air filter cleaned. It wasn't very dirty, Willy has done a good job. So far he has been the best bike mechanic I met. A friend came by and looked at my license plate and asks curiously! Where is Villarrica? In Paraguay about 8 650kilometer south. He was speechless.

Thursday April 30th I went back to the mechanic to get a few small details fixed, and to get ready for the road. The mechanic didn't want to get paid. I was surprised. I brought the bike home and went back to downtown. While strolling in high spirit I saw my doctor. He asked me about my health? I was surprised. Later a baker standing in front of his store, greeted me like an old friend. I can't remember seeing him before. We got in involved in a long conversation. Then he offers me a job. I have to think about it. It will be very hard to leave here. I love it here. I toured the city more. A Pakistani invites me for lunch at the local market. We talked about his wonderful gallery. Let's go and see it, he said We'll take the taxi to his small hidden gallery in a busy area. An tall husky artist, awaited us. He desperately asked the Pakistani. Have you sold any of my paintings yet? Could you give me an advance I have to feed my family with three little kids, he said. He gave him some money for the pictures he sold. It made me sick, especially after everything he just told me he owns. I look at all the paintings. He turns to me and invites me for one week vacation on the pacific coast. I have an apartment and we are going to have a great time. I laugh about him. I will think about it and leave. What a bastard. He pays the artist a nose water, that's all he can do for him and he invites me to a vacation. I am disgusted. Every night Nelly and her sister ask me about my day. Very interested they listen to my stories. Nelly says disappointed. I never have such luck. Are you going? Are you taking his invitation? I laugh, of course not. He is a liar. How do you know? Easy, if he really had so much money, then he wouldn't drive in a taxi. He only wants to sleep with me. Well from now on I pass the guys on to you, Nelly I said. A man asked me to ride with him on his bike. Showing me now proud his motorcycle, he was. I thanked him. It must be my dark blond hair and my blue eyes, that I get hit on all the time. Nelly couldn't understand, why I didn't go with him? I was five minutes away from home and I have a bike, too. Right behind you. I could feel his one track mind. Everybody laughs. I brought life to their dull Lives. It will be very hard, when I really leave here. Everybody is so good to me.

May 1st a national holiday, like Germany, we wait for Frank. He is a good guy, humorous, dating Nelly for years without getting serious. We gave him a hard time. He shows up, Nelly drives with him. Sereneida the younger sister rides with me. We plan to drive to San Isidro. It's a curvy road. We are all excited. We are faster than him, from time to time I look in the rear mirror for Frank. I can't see him. Disturbed we stopped and waited, no Frank. We turned around to look for him. There he is, his bike parked on the side of the road. We laugh for a second before asking concerned, what's wrong? The engine doesn't start, he said. What can we do? A man comes to help. He suggests to bring it to his house and we'll have a look. Relieved we follow this mechanic. He lives only five blocks away. We tow the bike. Jokingly I say to Frank, you have many tools and many problems. I have no tools and little problems. We all laugh. The helpers wife invites us to fresh squeezed grapefruit juice. It is delicious in the heat. He has a small home with a big cemented backyard. Now we get to work, trying to get the engine started. All efforts stay fruitless. The wife invites us for lunch. It was very good. We all thanked them. We had no choice to walk back to San Jose pushing his bike in disappointment. On the way back the oil starts leaking from my cylinder head For a moment I wished Willy the mechanic would be here to fix the bikes for good. Frank has constant problems, compared to mine. I feel lucky with my Brazilian made Honda. In the evening we sit around and needle Frank for dating Nelly for so long, but he doesn't want to get married. We know Nelly would love to have a family. You have to get out in public, meet more people. I encouraged her. Frank is insecure in the late 20's and Nelly is 28. He will make a decision or he will loose you. We all laugh. We are a happy crowd.

  The next morning Frank shows up in white pants and a red shirt. Wow, what a surprise. I was listening to the radio, enjoying myself. Together we drive to a mechanic who he knows in the mountain. What a fabulous view, but nobody was home. We go to another mechanic to get my cylinder head fixed. We return to the house. Albero is there with four men of the syndicate of agriculture talking business. Elith and Sereneida are both hyper they learned it from Juan. We made fun of everybody and telling jokes. We all had a good time After we ate, I drove Albero the big husky man on my bike to the bus terminal.

  May 3rd a Sunday. I went to see the parade. The marching civil guardian. They have no military here. It was fun, I took pictures. Then to the small zoo called Bolivar. I strolled through the cultural park listening to bands of live music. I was enjoying myself, as men were inviting me to go home with them. I tell them I am not looking for a man.

I just want to go home. Nelly came at the same time. Wet, too She returned from San Isidro after ten days of rain. That wasn't a vacation I shared her disappointment.

May 4th my last dental appointment. I was so happy. In the last six weeks I saw more doctors offices than ever before. At. night I talked to uncle Sam. An intelligent man, he traveled to many countries. He warns me to be careful, there are many thieves out there. Colon came and brought the prisoners from Spain and mixed them with the Indians. I haven't seen the pacific or the Atlantic coast. I wanted to explore more. Especially the unspoiled Atlantic coast with a small town Limon, which was hot, humid. I love the heat. It is hard to get there, you have to travel by train and predominantly blacks are working the plantations. That didn't excite me to much. The pacific coast is taken over from tourists and Americans. A long windy road leads to the coast, and I decided not to go plus the Stevens are waiting. The closer I got the slower I traveled, he said. It took the wind out of my sail, well tomorrow I will be in Nicaragua I say happily. I promised to be careful.

May 5th today I am leaving. It is very hard for me to take off, but my inner soul tells me to continue. I am way behind my schedule and I stayed long enough living, with Nelly and her sisters. Deep in my thoughts, I pack my belongings on the bike. Nelly shows up with her brother. He is medium height, husky and no hair. I greet them, I was surprised to see them. In this house people are coming and going at all hours. He apologized for his baldness. He had cancer and lost his hair during chemo therapy. I told him, don't worry. You look like Kojak without a lollipop. We all laughed hard. Both asked me intensely to stay longer. I deny. You need the bed for your brother, so he doesn't sleep on the floor. He was a sympathetic man in his mid thirty's. They would love for me to stay longer, entertain them with my daily stories. I just knew better. Time to continue on

America: Final Destination

my trip. I shake my head, and deny to stay. I thanked them several times for everything and their friendship. I started the motor, and turn around to wave. I left the city driving north. Where is the sun? I follow the sun and sing " on the road again." free like a bird. My heart is light, in one way, heavy on the other to leave my friends behind. Loneliness overcomes me. I already miss them, while driving through coffee and banana plantations to the border. A flat tire brings me back to reality. I made it to a gas station. I get it fixed and continue driving a lot uphill noticing my rear tire is blocking. I stop to realize my rear brake is blocking. I am upset. One problem after another here in nowhere. I look around. There ahead I see a bus station and men come over to help, but nobody has tools. They shake their heads that I have no tools on me. You are very careless to travel without tools they scolded me. Yes, I admit guilty. Here comes the bus. I shout with deep concerns. The bus driver frowns as he listened to me. He as well scolds me out. I thanked him for his lecture. That however it doesn't fix my problem I admitted depressed. Harshly he answers, there is another bus coming behind me shortly. He has tools. I thanked him. I waited for the second bus. The driver was a little friendlier. He got out the bus, loaned me two tools. I relieved loosened the rear brake, while two men held the bike. The bus driver looks astonished at us, asks the men are you together? No, they are just helping out. I thanked everyone for their help, I fixed the problem. They looked at me confused. I was happy. Singing on the road again. God sent me his angel to help. I was grateful for it. He is watching over me. He has his hands over me. The border. Stamped my passport for exit. Everybody is very polite and friendly. I asked for a glass of water. It is very hot outside. No problem says the understanding officer. He brings me a glass cold water. I drank it slowly. We talk nicely. All of a sudden the door opens. An officer enters, and looks at me.

Then he asks me for my passport. In the same voice I give back that my passport is already stamped. He demands unfriendly to see my passport. I am the boss. He looks at my visa. You overstayed your visa. Five US dollar. My invisible hat lifts from anger. Explaining him in detail. I got sick and had several doctor appointments. The boss didn't give up. He wanted five dollars. I wasn't willing to give him money. Then in my anger I remembered. I have a appointment card with me. I show the stubborn boss. That I have another appointment coming up. Which I will miss. He looks at it critically, finally he lets me go. Promising myself not to ask for water in an office again. Outside deep in my thoughts a casually dressed man demands from me 14.50 colon I told him I have no money. He tells me firmly, every tourist has to pay. I got mad. I asked him to close his eyes. What do you see? Nothing. That's what you get. I paid nothing for nothing. He laughs and we talk for a while. Think one hungry coyote after another.

Nelly and I overlooking a volcano in the background in the National Park - Volcano Poa

View of a lake in the National Park

Nelly and Frank at her house

Juan at Nelly's house in San Jose

Frank had engine trouble with his blue Honda in the rear.
My red Honda is in the front with Sereneida on the left,
Nelly next to her

Frank and I at the mechanic's garden

Sereneida (left) and Elieth at their home in San Jose

Albero and me on my motorcycle on the way
to the bus station

NICARAGUA

The best I continue driving in this hot desert. All a sudden I hear a whistle blowing. I ignore it. Sorry I take no hitch hikers. Then I hear two more whistle. I look in my rear mirror I see a green dressed man standing in the middle of the road. What does he want? A speeding ticket? Slide down my back (kiss my ass) A road barrier brings me to stop. A young federal instructs me to park my bike at the parking lot. I drive into a huge empty parking lot wondering what do I do now. I stopped and look around. A small skinny man came running with a big sombrero almost as big as him. Did I wake him up from his lunch nap in the shade. He smiled from ear to ear at me, like he just got a big present. I look at him calmly, waiting to hear what he wants from me. Continuously smiling he asks? Are you alone? No, I am with my bike and god. He busted out laughing. Here we stood in the heat, a burning sun. I laughed with him. What is this here? I ask him. Inspection he says. Sarcastically I ask, so you are inspecting my bike? No, go to immigration. Where? He pointed it out. Will you be watching my bike? He promised he would. I enter the building and see two young guys sitting behind counters working in slow motion. No air conditioner here. I stood waiting in line, watching them work. In two days they get more done then in one. I wished I had a book to read, while I was waiting. A middle aged man got behind me. Nobody talked. It was hot, sticky uncomfortable. The line moved slowly I turned around and asked the man, are you going through Nicaragua? Yes. I was relieved. Could I follow you? Yes, he says surprised. What are you driving? A motorcycle. A motorcycle? He says surprised. We better put it into my truck there is plenty of room. I got called to the window. It's the yellow truck. Wait for me there. I nodded and handed my passport to the young officer. He looked through, hands it back. I go to the next window, he said, there is a stack of papers to fill out, he asks a few questions. I return to my bike. It stands alone. I am concerned. Where did the dwarf go with his oversize sombrero? He was suppose to watch my bike with my luggage. There I saw him coming across the parking lot. He asked did, you see the different stations? Yes. Where is the yellow truck? I asked him. His smile went away. What do you want? Why do you want to go with him? I told him. This is none of his business. He pointed at the yellow truck at the end of the parking lot. Did you see the police? Police I questioned. You passed him coming here. The green one, I say humorous. Did you get a paper from him? I saw him doing his gymnastic, I didn't stop. The dwarfs face got concerned you have to go back and see him. I am not driving one meter back, I declared stubborn. Our discussion went on. He convinced me I had no choice. I left the bike next to the yellow truck and walked to see the policeman. He was waiting for me in the middle of the road. Didn't you see me? He asks harshly. Yes, I did. I thought you were selling hot dogs or lottery tickets at the booth, but I whistled three times. Continues the policeman mad. Yes, I heard you and thought you make your lunch exercise and you would give me a ticket for speeding. Silently he listened to me. He responds enough of the jokes. Now we get serious. This is a police under control and you have to pay $20. What $ 20? I say shocked, for what? Every vehicle has to pay $ 20. I told him in dry humor. I would like to earn my money that fast. Our discussion went on. I stood my ground, and refused to pay him one penny. Finally I had enough and walked away and left him standing in the middle of the road. I walked back. A young soldier at the road barrier pesters me about the police paper. Then he reads the law to me. I look at him from top to bottom. Seriously I tell him. You think a lot about yourself. You believe everybody falls to their knees and kisses your feet. Angry I continue. Your country is the biggest thief on god's earth. You get financial help from Germany and from the rest of the world. Now you want more. Not from me. I unleashed my anger on him and went back to the immigration office looking for the truck driver. He was there and told me to get in line again. What is it? Just get in line. So I stood there. One officer checks my passport again, where is the receipt from the police? I don't have one and I refuse to pay it. He rolled his eyes, showing it to his coworker. He told me you have to pay 20 $ and exchange 60 $ in Cordobas. How much is this in your local money? He points at a man close to me receiving several huge stacks of money. Each stack is approximately 30 centimeter high, all that? He nodded his head. I didn't bring a shopping bag, could I exchange less? No, what do I do with thousands of worthless Cordobas? It is that dirty, you can't even use it as toilet paper. I got a smile from these young skinny officers. All were my age and younger and telling me what to do? I had a fit, I refused to exchange that much. I prefer to keep 60$ it fits easily in my pocket. From both sides I was seriously advised the officers and the truck driver. You have to exchange the money or otherwise they don't let you into the country. I had to think about this. The truck driver sitting behind me on a chair, holding his hands in front of his face. Make up your mind. The disgruntled officers got more frustrated. We close at four o'clock or be back tomorrow at eight a clock. The driver says again to me. Pay or we unload the bike. I didn't want that. I knew he wanted to get into the country today, so did I. So I did my last strike. What do you need again? There was a lot of tension and frustration.

Exchange 60$ in Cordobas or just pay 20$ and we give you a receipt. Without a number as soon I leave you throw in the basket and the money goes in your pocket. I was fighting these guys to the teeth. We are closing in a few minutes. Alright I will exchange the money and get a bag. However I needed to use the bathroom and get the money. He knew what I meant. The officers three or four of them were visibly relieved You can go behind the building, it's safe there and come back. They counted the money for me. He made a comment. I understand everybody is afraid of you. They do what you ask them to do. I am not afraid of you. Your nose is in the middle of the face like everybody else. Everybody was speechless. Relieved with a little smile he handed my passport to me with a paper. The truck driver mumbles to me, you could have saved the arguments with them. You still had to exchange the money. Smiling I said. I was good for them. To put them in their place. The road barrier is closed. Happily I say, but the soldiers are still here and they will let us in. We drive up to the barrier. The soldier standing in formation lowers the flag. We are waiting for a young soldier to travel with us. He has to make sure we are not selling anything in the country. The ceremony is over. The barrier opens as well our mood. The soldiers run together starring at the truck cabin. Who is that? Why did we work overtime today? It was well past four o'clock. Some angry faces, some smiling faces. I smiled back. It's me! One young soldier gets in the cabin. We drive off, very relieved into the country. The pan American highway leads through cheerless desert. In a distance I see a small lake, we were hardly speaking. For the night we stopped at a big fenced in parking lot just for trucks. At a typical restaurant with a straw roof we had some dinner. We had Fish, rice and beer. It was good. Mariano the truck driver let me sleep in his cabin. He sleeps on the seat. He is a very good man. He talks a little about himself, but that's OK. In Costa Rica he sat in a restaurant. A girl came over and said, I like your T-shirt. He took off his T-shirt and gave it to her. He is a very good man and sympathetic. He drives for years from Guatemala to Costa Rica. Along the coast its quiet. The terrorists are more inland. I was very relieved, after all the fear they forced on me and war stories I've been told. They scared me. Relieved I fell asleep that night. It was a warm night. Early in the morning we drive to the city of Managua. We get there early. Mariano is in search of a replacement part. I stand around and watch how the city awakes. A train arrives with mostly open wagons. Lots of people sit on it with their goods. The train stops, like on a command everybody gets up at the same time grabbing their baskets. Jumping off the wagon walking in different directions. It is a colorful sight. We are parked next to a gas/repair station. Mariano puts up his hammock in the shade, while the mechanic works. Later I hear a mess and singing over a loudspeaker. It's morning. I wanted to explore the city. I see a huge open air market, but the majority of booths, are closed. The selection is poor. I see nothing interesting there. The prices are expensive for locals. I walked and seen watermelons are for sale. I ask politely for the price. The woman looks at me with disgust and hisses " la gringa" wouldn't sell me anything. The husband smiled at me, and gladly sold two pieces to me. Mariano was still napping. It was hot and humid. When he woke up, I asked him would you like some watermelon? He would. Wait I have to go and buy some. I ate yours. The man was disturbed that I came back for more. I explained it would be for my friend. Unfriendly he sold me a couple of more slices You can't buy a whole, just a slice. That was an eye opener. It's a communist country. I learn there are lots of German engineers and teachers here. With them, they developed the country. For the night we parked in a fenced trailer park. Dinner was rice, beans and meat, three times a day. I was grateful we got to eat anything at all. I didn't care for the country and their politics. One positive observation was the few vehicles on the road. Will I come back? If it becomes a democratic country, may be. Only may be. The next morning we walked to immigration. A small little booth along the road with white curtains. It looks like a confession booth. You couldn't see the person sitting in the dark. I had to bite my tongue I thought that was to funny. He asked a lot of questions. Slowly he annoyed me. I forced myself to be polite. When will he stop I wondered? Repeatedly he asked. Where are you going? I told him to Guatemala. He wouldn't let go. You are going to America. I wanted to tell him its none of your business, but I knew better. I bit my tongue and said, look I traveled with a truck and the driver is waiting for me. Let me go and give me my passport. Again silence from the booth. That guy made me very angry, but I didn't show it. Then he asked me for a paper. Luckily I saved it. I handed it to him. At slow motion he hands me passport through the little window. Come back soon. I grabbed my passport and ran to the truck. Mariano was waiting for me. Out of breath I told him he almost wouldn't let me go. Did you tell him you are going to Guatemala? Yes, I did.

HONDURAS

The officials everywhere wanted money. One window wanted even more money, the next window wanted even more money. The day traders for money exchange hang on us like parasites. I exchanged only a little money, since in a few hours we would be on the border. The coast highway is very dry. It's summer. It's depressing. Mariano explains that the whole pacific coast is like that. On the Atlantic coast its green with virgin rainforest. There are lots of animals and the Americans. We had lunch. It was good, but the people were not very friendly. They don't eat much fruit and vegetables.

The border of Honduras

Pottery on display for sale

EL SALVADOR

The usual paperwork. No money for my bike, that was a pleasant surprise. Mariano exchanges his Cordoba's for a better rate than me. He teased me, you should have waited. I admitted my defeat. I lost some money on the other hand I had less to carry. We all laughed. Mariano has lots of friend here. We have to go to custom, in every country to get the truck fumigated. It was hot and humid outside their offices. I talked and joked with the officials. Some have not much to do. Central America is like a cow. Everybody is milking her, everybody wants a glass of milk. Money to get in the country. Money to leave the country. We all laughed. I looked unsuccessfully for Mariano. Where is he? The truck is in the parking lot. I waited a long time for him. I started swearing. I feel like taking my bike out and keep driving, but Mariano would wait for me. I can't do that to him. I walked up and down the alley in the shade, a hot breeze was blowing. A policeman stops me. We started talking. I told him. I am waiting for Mariano. He is gone for a long time probably making push ups at his girl friends mattress. He laughs. We talk more, he shares his potato chips with me. We talk about the war. He thinks it is only a business. No war, no weapons, no business. The USA delivers the weapons, to the soldiers. I am amazed about his knowledge of this situation. Still no Mariano, angry I think, where he be? In a distance I see him coming. Impatiently I ask him. Where have you been? He says, he met colleges and they drank lemonade. I am suppose to believe that? I gave him another look. I felt bad for a moment for my bad thinking. I'm just glad he is back. I was relieved something bad could have happened. We continue driving through the desert. In San Miguel we stopped at a restaurant. It's evening. We met his friends Tico Edwin and the police drank beer with salt and ate cerviche. Lots of jokes and legends were told. I just listened. While music is blasting in the background. Later we had chicken and potatoes with more beer. Later we went to bed. I woke up at night with a burning thirst. I steal myself out of the truck to not wake Mariano in his bed cabin. I went to the bathroom to drink water. The faucet is dry, not a single drop. In the garden the faucet is dry, too. I am in shock. No water anywhere. It is a warm night, a breeze is going. My faithful water bottle is empty, usually I am so good to keep it filled. I break my head. Where to get water for my burning thirst, and dry mouth, dry throat. I couldn't find any. Defeated I return to the truck, thinking about other things, while falling asleep. In the morning I wake up cold and shivering. My thirst was gone. We continue crossing bridges, always guarded with soldiers. Later on we see a modern bridge blown up. It happened just recently. Two bridges in the value of 25 million dollars. A cold shower is running down my spine. I just imagine if we were on the bridge, when it blew up. It crosses a deep river. We take a detour. Which puts us on the train track. This adventure just wouldn't stop. I looked at Mariano scared and said I hope no train is coming. He said it wouldn't. To my right homes are burnt and bombed. It was clear to me. War is terrible. This went on for miles and miles. I hoped we get there in peace. The president from El Salvador and Honduras doesn't care about the towns. Lots of illiterate, they can't read or write. The average family has ten children, but are very poor. One banner reads: Protect our land from the bombs of the terrorists. The people are very poor and frightened.

Border of El Salvador

The Pacific Coast in Central America

GUATEMALA

May 8th the officers were very friendly to me. When they saw my German passport, custom officer and vehicle inspector in exchange gave me a lot of problems, real assholes. My patient runs out. Angry I ask three times for his boss. He just sat there sullen. His neighbor told him go to the boss. He got up with my papers and I followed him to his boss to the room next door. The boss listens to his story. Politely the boss asks, what nationality is the passport? Quickly I respond German. Surprised he looked at me, and says everything is good. I thanked him and followed the asshole officer to his desk. He stamps my passport and asks about my bike. I think to myself. This guy thinks a lot about himself, why not right away. Everybody in the office smiles and wishes me a good trip. I thank everybody. I left with a successful smile. Meet Mariano he is done with his paper trail. We continue. Green mountains, plantations a real paradise. There is a volcano Pacaya where white smoke is rising to the sky. The volcano is active. Mariano pointed it out. He is as well my tour guide. For years he travels back and forth. Guatemala to Costa Rica. He lived for a while in

America. For many years, he didn't like it. He asks me why are you going there? These people are so stupid. They don't know where central America is. To them it borders with Texas.I was astonished. I am going to see friends in San Francisco. They are waiting for me, I said heartfelt. You live in a beautiful country. I fell in love. The mountains get higher and the air gets fresher. There is a Safari Club next to the main road with animals from

Africa. It belongs to a rich man. We stop at a fruit stand and buy several kind of fruits, some I didn't even know. What a paradise. One looks like an avocado, but the skin is brown, the meat is reddish. Skeptical I bite into it. It has a big pit in the middle. Mariano looks at me questioning. It tastes good, I say surprised. He made me taste all the fruits, until my stomach almost busted. So many kinds of fruits I never knew. He was amused. He asks again why do you want to go to America? The people are very arrogant. They don't know where Guatemala is. He insisted that I spend at least four weeks in his beautiful country. I love it here. The quetzal Bird is the national animal of liberty. If he gets caged, he dies of unhappiness, just like me. I need my freedom. The Germans are welcomed here. He tells me proudly.

The German president was here shortly before me, visiting the country. He promised to help finance an asphalt the road to the German colony to the north. He gave 200 police cars BMW's and Mercedes as a present. He is a good guide. What good timing. I wasn't aware of it. That's why everybody on the border was so friendly. Mariano nodded. In the evening still driving, he asks me. What are we having for dinner? Quickly I answer. Fruits. We have lots of fruits. He looks at me grimly. We are not monkeys. We have to eat hearty food. We stop at a restaurant. We found a parking lot on the street for his long trailer. The restaurant is typically decorated. Everything is so nice. Heavy wooden table have colorful tablecloths. We sit down. Mariano knows the kind waitress. Everybody in the country is friendly, polite and helpful. He ordered steak, quesadilla, mixed salad and beer. While eating. He says, thank you. That we had no sex together. I almost fell from my chair. Forgot to eat for a moment. He sees that, continue eating he says. I have a girlfriend in El Salvador. We have a child together and I support her. A hot flash went through my head, my humorous thought was right. A friend showed up. He joined us with a beer talking for a while. He has a 250 Suzuki. Mariano asks him to bring me to the doctors house. I thanked him several times for guiding me in the dark cold night. I would have had a hard time finding this place in the dark night. In the suburb of Guatemala city. We knocked on the door. The doctors wife Arciela was home and I handed her the letter from Ricardo. She was surprised and let me in. We sat until midnight talking about the Mayan.

  May 9th doctor Carlos introduced himself. A polite, pleasant man working long hours. We had breakfast together inclusive beans, tortillas, eggs, salsa and coffee. We talk. They have two small children. We go to a catholic church. It's gorgeous with lots of gold. Afterwards we visit the Mercado and I buy myself a typical outfit. A hand embroidered blouse and skirt with the quetzal bird.

  May 10th Sunday. The doctor tells me he is in a social democratic party, consults and helps the poor. They pay him as they can. Which is little. He has many clients and works long hours. Life is harsh and fast in the city. In their inside patio they have a big basin tub out of cement. It is always filled with water. At night the water gets turned off. Rationing. The wife is very educated, too. She works at the University, but for now mostly stays home taking care of the baby. I was happy, they let me stay with them for a few days. We go to Antigua, a Spanish city. They are very religious built in 1549. We visited the cathedral ruins. It was amazing how they built it. Ten million Guatemalans people live in Los Angeles. The university was closed. We saw the Palacio Grande police. I looked at artic rafts, handcrafts, and clothes. We had lunch in the Mercado. Chicken, avocado, tortillas and soda. Then we took the bus high up the mountain. There we walk around and eat sweets. Dulce de chiverry and figs. Guatemala was the capital of central

America before Belize, Honduras, El Salvador and Mexico got independent.

May 11th Monday family Gomez, Carlos sister arrived. It is a holiday and Carlos had a day off. Together we go to lake Amatitlan. We take a boat ride and I admire the view. The big lake is surrounded with mountains. A beautiful setting the sun is shining. It was fun but fresh here. The gondola is closed on Monday. We are all disappointed. So we stroll through the open air market. Everybody is offering cooked fish lying open on a platter. We buy one cooked fish and one cooked chicken. Happy we all sit on a picnic table eating, and talking. One notices the fish has a bitter taste. The sister turns the fish over and with her fork she pulls the baked skin off. Worms came out, crawling all over. We almost threw up and we drank more beer to kill everything we just ate. Carlos, his sister and I went back to the vendor showing her the fish. Chewing her out. It is reckless to leave the fish so long out and the flies lay their eggs in it. She protested. I am a doctor and I will call the health department. She gave Carlos his money back. We returned to the family table. They all awaited the news. What did the vendor say? Carlos shared the news. We cleaned the table and in a group we walked through the half closed market due to the holiday. All the fish had disappeared, none was for sale any more. Interesting most women here are only 1.40 -1.50 meter tall. I feel tall overlooking all the heads. I am only 1.60 meter tall. Good people. We went to see her sister, she is a nurse. A good person. She lives alone, her husband works in another town. She made coffee and food for us. We had a wonderful time. As a nurse she makes 450 quetzal about 180 Us dollar. Arciela makes 950 quetzal about 380 US dollar at the university, her housekeeper earns 60 quetzal about 24 Us dollar with room and board in the city.

May 12th Tuesday morning we went to the mechanic to change my rear brakes and cylinder. Nice people. I paid five quetzal, two Us dollar. From here I visited the dentist, and visited the tourist office getting a map showing many historical sites. I was very happy. So much to see and explore.

May 13th Wednesday morning I got up and bought bread. I took off to the Atlantic coast as I came off the mountains I peeled my clothes like a banana. It was getting hot, humid and the land became flat. I visited Mayan ruins in Quirigua along the highway next to the banana plantations. There is not much known about the history. However many locals were peddling green bananas very cheap. I bought two bunches to support them and my appetite for fruits. From here I continued to Rio Dulce and San Cristobal crossing a big river on a big bridge. The river flows into the vast (wide) open Atlantic ocean. A stunning scene. Over the bridge to the left the roads leads to the ruins of San Cristobal. The Spanish had a fort here to control. Who is coming or going into the country. With my bike I was flying and drove into the fort with my eyes searching for the ruins. Several tourists were picnicking or laying on a blanket on the grass. While searching with my eyes for these ruins I almost drove over a couple laying on a blanket. I stopped right at their blanket. Their heads flew up, they turned around. Shocked and outraged they looked at me. I smiled and said "hey" and then asked. So these are the ruins? Pointing straight ahead. My spirit was high and I felt on top of the world. The couple just complained to me. I apologized for my reckless driving, but it was funny. I backed up I looked around for the castle. I continued driving north. At first the road was good. People advised me to fly to Tikal. They told me the road is very bad. I smiled. I have a bike I insisted to drive. This went through my head while driving up green mountains overlooking yellow valleys. It was so peaceful and breath taking. I stopped for a while to capture this view. For a moment I thought I was in Germany. Wonderful and untouched by nature to the eye. I could have stayed here I thought dreaming, but I was on my way to Tikal. I continued driving uphill, later it leveled out. I wondered where did the road go? To the left was a huge mountain, to the right straight downhill and in front of me a rockslide. No road. Well, I'll just drive over these loose rocks in hope to find a road again. It was a challenge and I drove and drove. After a few minutes a sort of road appeared. It looked more like a plowed field than a road. Very rough. This went on for hours I hardly saw a vehicle any vehicle on the road besides me. In s small village I stopped to buy a soda. The friendly people were surprised. That I was driving to Tikal. That's the only road going there, I replied smiling and in bad humor. In the afternoon I found a motel for the night. My whole body was sore and swollen. I could hardly walk, every step hurt. I found a small restaurant even eating hurt. I went back to the hotel and took a shower. It felt like needles on my body. I cried from pain and went straight to bed. The next morning I got up surprisingly most of the pain and swelling was gone. That was the worst road I have been on for a long time. The road to Tikal from now on was better. Along the asphalt road I saw a blond haired tall guy walking and hitch hiking. I stopped asking him. Where do you want to go? Tikal. Me too I said laughing. Hope on, it felt good to be with my own kind. Martin is from New Zealand and missed the bus so he started walking. To his luck I came along. We joked. We came to a checkpoint. I stopped. The men are laughing, because I am driving and a long legged guy behind me. We laugh together, because Martin could push the bike and make it go faster. We pay our entrance fee. Tikal is actually a park with Mayan ruins, and well preserved. The Mayans are proud of their heritage. We visited the museum together.

Martin knew a lot about the Mayans. I didn't and felt a little embarrassed. He explained the history and artwork. Actually I felt good to run into him. He became my tour guide. In the museum I could feel the peoples spirit. The huge ruins in the rainforest where very impressive, amazing what these Mayans did thousand of years ago. I was eager to learn their history. We enter a huge area. The size of a soccer field with two temples facing each other. One on the left. One at the right. It was so impressive, so huge and so tall. I felt like an ant looking up to an giraffe. We walked hundreds of stairs lined with a chain to hold on. The breeze up here felt good. I thought for a moment what must these kings felt, overlooking this huge field, looking over to the other tower. What went through their head? The breeze up here felt good compared to the hot humid climate at the bottom. All day I felt back in time when the Mayan king lived here. Why did they abandoned the city? I spent all day walking around looking at different buildings. It is well kept and very impressive. In the afternoon I found Martin again waiting by my bike. He properly got tired of my poor English. We had a beer, talked about the day and I gave him a ride back to catch his flight. It was a delight to be with a white person with blue eyes for a change I stayed the night in Flores. A small town by a big beautiful lake Petén.

May 15th I slept well. The sun is already strong. The drunks are strolling in for their room as I take off to drive around the lake taking pictures. Then off to Sebol south west of Tikal a small Mayan ruin setting in the rainforest. Late morning in the woods I approached a small woman carrying wood in a nylon sack on their back attached to a headband. This is so amazing to have the strength. These people amaze me. I asked her for water. She looks at me shy, asking coffee, coffee? I just nodded and followed her into her simple home. She had a huge pot on the stove with a big wooden ladle, she is serving me coffee. To me it looked and tasted like warm water with a few coffee beans. I was grateful and thanked her several times. I used to have a water bottle with me. I left it with Mariano. He learned water is better for thirst than soda. The very basic. The dirt roads are often very bad. All flat terrain set in green tropical rainforest. A real paradise. On the way I see a boy riding a horse with a simple harness no mouth piece. He has two three horses behind him. One carries bananas the other carry firewood. The horses here are used to carrying freight or pull carriages. Homes along the road are very bad and the people are very poor, but happier than the city folks. Its always flat on a straight road lined with rainforest on both sides. This paradise invited me to dream. I was in heaven. Just me, my bike, and nature. After a short drive the road made a curve and the road ended on a beautiful wide river. Curving around unspoiled just like a painting. I was stunned. It was so beautiful, deep blue water impossible to pass by motorcycle. I stood a few minutes stunned from the beauty of nature and at the same time concerned about how to cross the river. All of a sudden from nowhere came a boat to shore. I was relieved, a gift from heaven. Did god and the angels hear me? The men in the boat said something I didn't understand. They helped me to put the bike in the motorboat and we tuckered across the river. It was such a idyllic settings it took my breath away. The short ride was priceless. Nature at its best. Amazingly behind the forest emerged a vibrant town. It surprised me, how hidden it was. It was a fast paced town. Everybody was in a hurry. Where I am? Wondering to myself. A couple of guys tried to pick me up and teased me while walking with me. I went into a bakery to shake them off. Quickly I had to find Sebol to get away from here I didn't like that town. I came to the ruins.

    The grounds keeper at the ruins was moody and not very social. I asked him about the carvings on the tombstones. He didn't care to share his knowledge. That was disappointing. I asked him for some water to drink. He came back with a cup and showed me proudly how he gathers rainwater in a big container. The water tasted awful and I was so thirsty so I drank it gratefully, but I didn't want seconds. I Thanked him and continued driving through the forest on very bad roads. At an intersection I debated to go right to the German colony, Coban. That's where the quetzal the bird of paradise lives. Here are no signs or advisory and hardly anyone on the road. I didn't take a chance went to the left. In the rain season the trucks destroy the dirt road by plowing their way through. President Kohl from Germany gave 40 million to asphalt the road to Coban. In a way I felt sorry, than nature is totally destroyed. Traveling is not challenging any more, the adventure is gone. The people are fighting for their freedom. Before there was a lot of violence. The military took everything. They don't want to work only to get paid. I stay overnight in Las Casas. In my motel my neighbor is a mix. German French and Indian. He is a very tall man, a good person and sharing a lot about his life. He is a member of the Christian democratic party since 1966, separated from his wife. Who knows where she lives? He is a mechanic and has his land plants rice, corn and beans. When he comes to town he always stays here. He lived a short time in Hamburg Germany in 1948. I felt his loneliness and enjoyed his story. He got up from the table and said wait here. He came back with a cowboy hat and handed it to me, saying: I can't believe you drove these bad roads. Take this as a gift. My admiration to you. I was deeply touched from this simple hard working man. His hands showed it. I thanked him sincerely. It was like a gold medal to me. The owner had a blue fronted Amazon parrot. I looked at him with sorrow. Jacos loss was still deep in my heart, but at the same time I enjoyed seeing parrots as pets.

May 16th I travel through rolling hills burned forest cleared for farming and grazing. They grow sugarcane, corn, rice, beans and grazing cattle's. It is called new the land. My heart hurts to see this crime on nature. Destroying the ecosystem of the rainforest. The roads are bad, often filled with stones, rocks. Which the trucks tear up in bad weather. The women are shy. They don't want to talk to strangers. They sent a boy or a man usually to answer my questions, for directions, a motel or place to eat. Their wooden homes with palm leaves for roof look good, very basic. The Mayans are very hard working. Carrying incredible amounts of material on their back holding with a forehead band. How can they do that, without breaking their neck? I respect these people a lot. Later in nowhere I eat my last can of tuna from Peru, with stale bread. It was better than none. Standing here on a road in nowhere in the forest. I was content. I love it here. Love the tropical rainforest, threatened to return to the city, but my toothache didn't go away.

In the villages are often military posts and road barriers. They deal with drugs and sell them to America. The democracy of the rich. Along the river I see several women kneeling down and washing clothes with a palm tree leave as a hat. I found it very original and amusing. You have to be creative. I smiled at them. It is very hot in Rio Dulce back on asphalt roads. Its very curvy going uphill I passed several trucks with trailers. I took on to pass when a double trailer pulled out in front of me going uphill. I hoped he would pass the other double trailer and pull over. He wouldn't I grew impatient and set on to pass him sharing the same lane. The road had two lanes each directions. I passed the truck half way the road goes into a curve uphill. To my horror two huge trailer trucks in duo are coming down the hill. I had nowhere to go. I open the throttle trying to pass the truck on the left. The draft coming downhill and a draft from two trailers going uphill wouldn't allow me. I was sandwiched for a moment between two trucks and their suction. One pulling me uphill, the other downhill. My heart almost stood still. I tucked down to the tank. Balancing my bike being battered around in their draft. We were so close to both sides that only a finger space was left. I felt any moment I will be pressed to the truck be as flat as a postage stamp. There was no room at all. No time to be scared. I just drove, keeping an eye on the road. It seemed forever. When the downhill draft eased I was able to pass the uphill double trailer truck. Very relieved I passed the truck still driving uphill. That was a long pass. Happily driving soaked in sweat I hear a police siren. My heart sunk in my shoes. What does he wants now? I slowed down. The police on a motorcycle came next to me driving. He looks at me, and says mean. That was a dangerous pass. You could a been killed. Cool unimpressed, I say. Some people die earlier others die later. A moment of silence. He dropped back. Then I saw him coming back in my rear mirror again. What is it now? A speeding ticket? He was really mad. I pulled over on top of the hill at the parking lot. I was mad at myself, thought how much will this ticket me cost? I stopped at the parking lot like told to with the motor idling. The policeman arrived, asking for my drivers license. My heart slipped in my shoes. I had the license in a pouch around my neck. I needed to take my helmet off to see the papers. The police face changed. I gave him my passport and driver license. He looked it over and then, looked at me. I was dressed in long pants, an old leather coat. He didn't expected to see a woman. He changed, his voice became friendlier. He said. I won't give you a ticket, but promise me to drive slower and more careful. I did. I drove slower not passing anymore trucks, since I got away with my blue eyes. No ticket. I was happy. He was right. It was a dangerous pass, but I got stuck. At 6:30pm I arrived at the house in Guatemala city. Ariciela was surprised. You are back so soon. My tooth bothers me. The neighbor came over to hear about my trip. I drove from here to Quiringa Mayan ruins They have the best ornaments. Next to a banana plantations -export for America - San Felipe -Tikal -Sebol- Las Casas -Rio Dulce. They were impressed about my trip.

May 17th Sunday we go together to the market to buy fruits and veggies. One man samples a pineapple. He gave everybody a piece except to me. Carlos asked the vendor one piece for her. La gringa? No Germany I reply. We all laugh and hands me a piece. It was a nice day. We had a good time. Went to bed early.

May 18th we go together to the museum. It was closed. We continue to see the handcraft market, nice crafts.

In the afternoon I see the dentist. He has a happy face. What is he thinking? He gives me anesthesia to pull my tooth. The pressure was gone. I went back to the house to sleep early.

May 19th I slept in, taking it easy to let the wound heal. Arciela is jealous about me. I ask her? Why don't you travel, get to know other countries? But the children. Carlos travels a lot. He likes parties, loves to talk.

He is the president of the syndicate.

May20th Wednesday I went to change the oil. One guy goes with me to buy a new battery. A sign in the store read: don't say everything you know, don't believe everything you hear, don't do everything you can, don't spend everything you have. I found it interesting. I went back to the house and washed my bike with the neighbors help. We got done faster. These are good people. We visit the Archaeological and Ethnology museum. It is a very big exhibit of interesting Mayan cultures mainly. We spent several hours there. Tomorrow I'll leave. Its fabulous to travel the world, worry free.

May 21st Early Thursday I get my bags loaded. Together we have breakfast. Carlos can't believe I am leaving. It was hard to go. These people are so wonderful and kind. I couldn't thank them enough for everything. I am driving north to visit his sister in Huehuetenango. Passing wonderful scenery in the mountains. A checkpoint. A police reviews my paper then I get on a narrow, steep curvy road to Chichicastenango, 18 kilometers to the famous Indian market. I was sweating. It was worth the drive. The town has small homes clustered next to each other. The Indians wearing colorful traditional outfits. A real joy. One is prettier than the other. All Mayans carry their load on their back with a strap over their forehead. How can they do that? They must have a strong neck. This town and market is impressive. A church is close by, people sitting in front of it and pray. A boy offers to watch my bike for a small fee. I pay gladly him. Many beggars want money and they are everywhere. It was overwhelming. This is definitely a tourist town and many expect a handout. How shocking, I walk around and buy some fruit, a kid comes begging for money. The saleswoman looks curiously at me. I understand, she is selling fruit to make a living and the kid wants money for doing nothing. He continued pestering me, finally I handed him a banana. I bargained for a traditional jacket with quetzal birds on it. I return to my bike. The boy watching my bike asks, Where is Villarrica? Paraguay. Everybody around looks confused. I continue driving on the curvy road. People look wave at me, they are so friendly. They don't like gringos. The north Americans treat the Guatemalans bad. I come to Solacha and visit the market. I met a Colombian woman three hours from Cali. We talk for a long time. What a small world. I continued to lake Atitlan, the mirror lake as I came down the mountain to see the lake, it is very foggy so I turned around and drive straight to Huehuetenango. Late afternoon, I arrive at family Gomez's house. Carlos sister. They were happy to see me. We put my bike into their big enclosed patio. I was very tired. You will stay a long time with us, they declared to me. I agreed, and became part of the family.

May 22nd Friday. Early we leave for Quetzaltenango to visit their daughter attending college. On the way we stop in San Marcos and San Pedro to deliver cowhides for treatment. Augustin and Martha Gomez owns a butcher shop. His nephew makes shoe soles and the business stays in the family. The people work hard. Police control everything along the road. They are everywhere. I find them annoying. The mountains are so beautiful, but we overheated the motor. In a river Augustine gets water for the carburetor I found it hilarious. Better than burning up the engine, I said. Our treat of the day was bathing in thermal water. This is very healthy, Martha explains. The parents Augustin and Martha get a private bathtub. He is tall, slim about two meters plus, the wife is small curvy may be one meter forty-five. The daughter Maria twelve years old shares a private bathtub with me and her huge bed at the house. The hot water feels great I can even swim a little in there. It feels like a roman bathhouse. Refreshed and clean we drove home. We have Sausages for dinner. My favorite. Afterwards we sit together talking until late.

May 23rd Saturday after breakfast Ely, Paola and Carlos a friend and two Gomez sons in teenage years take off with me to Chantla looking for boots. I wanted new cowboy boots made in Guatemala. He says this leather is better than in Mexico. I got a pair for 30dollars, I was very happy and pleased, I got my pictures developed as well. I had lots of fun hanging out with the kids. I am about ten years older than them. I like their energy and karma. In the evening we went to a friends house. The husband had just died, friends and family members came to pay their respect. Nine days they kept the closed coffin. It was a small house in one room with dim light for the display. Most people go into the room, pray and leave, making room for others. I didn't understand the ceremony so I walk around and see a picture hanging on the wall in their living room. Mrs. Gomez approached me. That is him. He was in his thirties. Nosy I ask, how did he die? To much alcohol and fell off the horse, leaving five children behind. He also was beating his wife a lot. I commented in dry humor. She should be glad he is dead. Psst, you can't say that. I looked at the widow and her kids. All hard workers, you will be fine. Now you are free. No one could smile, because we are here to remember the dead husband. I shut up. It was a cold night and chilly in the house. I went to find their outdoor wood fired oven for baking bread. I followed the smell of fresh baked bread and the warm. I stood next to it, warming my bones. I love their bread. I felt for the widow and her kids.

May 24th We have breakfast pork, beans, cheese and tortillas. The coffee is hot water to me. With Paola(Maria) the youngest about my height I go to the bus terminal, together. Where her parents have a butcher shop selling meat to the travelers. We bring their lunch. We watch the farmers eat without silverware. They eat their beans rolled in a corn tortilla. Every meal is with tortilla. As dessert, coffee with a sweet roll. They open at five in the morning. Lots of people travel. We sell a lot of meat. They are known of good quality meat. They as well have a booth in the Mercado. Sunday and Thursday are the best days. I helped, it was educational. Afterwards we stroll the market. I love their big variety of fruits. There are so many kinds of Mangos alone. I was in heaven. At night it rained and I got a toothache again. I call the Stevens, Ray is mad at me. The closer you get to America, the slower you travel.

He was right, I admitted. I felt bad, but these people here are so wonderful. Life is good.

May 25th I visited the Mexican consulate. Nice people. He is a pharmacist. He drives a 500 Honda and loves to travel. We connected and talked for a long time. I learned in the town of Socaltenango used to live many Germans like in Coban. Many Indians live there with white skin, some have blue eyes and black hair. The Germans wanted to take away this area from Guatemala, and become independent just like the English with Belize. The Guatemalan president told them to get out. Then in 1982 through 1985 there were guerillas here. They were attacking and killing many people. With civilian patrol it took every man helped to chase them out. Now they have money, food and there land. The guerillas lived in the forest like Petén. That was my history lesson of the day. I went to three banks trying to exchange cash dollar, but everybody wants checks. This was hard to believe.

May 26th Tuesday every morning the husband Augustine makes breakfast. Today fried eggs fried onions and salsa. It was delicious. I was amazed. He cooks daily. Together we go to the market to their meat booth.

They do well. Everybody of the family helps. They have an elderly lady as cook. We like to tease her, because she complains a lot. However she is a good cook. My favorite dish was beef tongue in tomato sauce. Today she made cow foot soup (Caldo de Pata de Waka) with toasted vegetables. It contains a lot of gelatin. That was the best I ever ate. It was gourmet delicious. I praised her a lot. She was very proud of my compliments. I asked for the recipes she refused, but promised to make it again. At that time I watched her cooking and she opened up explaining the process. I shared with her my German cake recipes. Everybody loved it. A big pot is always on the stove. They add lime (calcium) to the water for cooking corn. It helps peeling the corn and than grinded it to make tortillas. All the work is done by hand. At two o clock in the afternoon Augustin, Martha, Maria and I drove to Ixtavacan to see cows. They came from Mexico, the exchange is cheaper, but the seller asks to much. He was very unhappy for not getting his price and the sale. We just left. The drive is nice, joyful seeing the Mayans to weave a blankets, it takes a month. They fasten it on top of the post. The other end with a pedal is tight around their back. Every village has their own design, that's how they identify themselves. The wool got expensive, explains the woman while talking to us. She is calm and relaxed, and continued weaving while talking to us. The poncho is very thick the hats have a banner. The sandals are from thick leather and the sole from old car tires. I found it hilarious. Everything gets recycled. They live in stone or adobe homes in the mountain. Cooking on woodstoves. They wash themselves in steam. By heating stones then pouring water on it. Its cold in the mountains. Its makes sense. They except new things into to their life while living their traditional live. They carry heavy loads on their back with a thick broad leather strap on their forehead instead of shoulder straps. They grow corn here. It has the best ground and climate. They work and work, barely enjoying life. I enjoy the outings with the family. They are wonderful tour guides and explain their customs.

  May 28th I went with the teenage boys to practice martial art. Japanese karate. They have a yellow belts. I practice Korean Taek won do and have a green belt. It is a good school. They have a couple of guests visiting for a week. A Mexican teacher, a five degree black belt and a Chinese instructor from Hong Kong. Both are excellent instructors very patient and agile. I had a good time. In the afternoon we all helped cleaning and cutting vegetables for the upcoming birthday party. I baked cakes. Were are all happy and joyful working into a cold night until eleven. There is no heater except the kitchen stove.

May 30th Saturday the long awaited day is here. Eric's 15th birthday. At six in the morning Paola/ Maria gets up like a rocket, waking me up. We share a king size bed. She went to wake up Eric on the couch, but there is no Eric. She went to his bed, touching the blankets. No Eric. She is in shock. Then I hear Paola screaming. I was up and running trying to find out what is going on. Eric was hiding in the bathroom and sneaking up on his sister from behind touching her shoulder, shouting. Surprise. Over breakfast we heard the story and we all laughed. It was Eric's special day. With fifteen you become an adult. For lunch we had chicken, and potato salad. For dessert pineapple and apple pie had baked I with whip cream. A special treat. In the afternoon we practiced karate at the studio. Tomorrow they will do a public demo in the town hall. Everybody is excited and nervous at the same time. In the evening many people came for the party. A happy gathering. Together we serve the food and then the coffee. We cut the cakes, everybody loved my cakes. Then the youth started dancing to the music and the adults started talking and drinking. A very happy time, even the dogs had a party. Cleaning all the plates. The youth went later to dance in Chantla, after the party was over. I went to bed it was late and cold.

May 31st Sunday morning I woke up with a hangover. So did everyone else. We all had breakfast together the whole family, brother, sister, etc. We talked about the party and the good time. Together we went to the bus terminal to bring lunch to the parents. There were so many people, good sales today. Augustin and Martha have been working early with their hangover. They both looked tired. We helped for a while. Then I ventured off to find mangos. Find red mangoes. There are so delicious. I love fruits, the vendors know me. Carmen the sister to

Martha is a very happy person and understands. At three in the afternoon we drive to the huge gymnasium to see the demonstration of a young Karate Club and the masters. Lots of people came to watch. The students did their demo first, than Jimmy spoke. He looks like Bruce Lee. I thought it was a good impressive speech. He respects Guatemala and you should respect the karate students. However some people whistled, shouted and protested. Jimmy ignored them and kept on speaking. I respected him for that alone. The students did their fighting form. I felt out of place and didn't do my forms. The audience had little sympathy. Then Jimmy did his performance fast and limber just like Bruce Lee. The students and me were breathless and excited. Our goal became to become like him. The highlights was when Jimmy pulled a car with his teeth. There was dead silence, everybody watched. Then applauded. The Mexican master broke with his forehead several blocks of real bricks. I took lots of pictures of their performances and sold him the film later. We exchanged addresses. I told him as well I don't want to have your head tomorrow. He just waved, I take a couple of Tylenol for pain. Both men impressed me for their good and fast techniques. It is cold we return to the house. It rains every afternoon. Martha and Augustin go to mess. The kids and me stay home. The phone rang. A friend comes over and the boys are going to the cinema. I asked polite say can I join? They were not thrilled, but I didn't want to be home alone. So I just tattered along. Half way there, they turn around saying it is a love movie trying to scare me away. I have money and by my way, I can see what you see. They bought their tickets and I was right behind them. The cashier looked puzzled when I purchased my ticket for Dienna. We sat in the middle close together. The cinema was near empty, but filled up fast, all men. I felt like a drop of milk in a coffeepot. Finally the light went out and the movie started. It was a long interesting sex movie. Half way through came a break, the light goes on all the eyes were on me. Now I realized I was the only woman here and the cinema was packed. I just ignored them all and waited until most of them got up to use the bathroom and return. My companions moved a couple of seats over not to be associated with me. I was fine, but a stranger moved close to me and asked me after the movie. How did you like the movie? I gave him my opinion. It was a good classic movie. Here women don't come to see these kind of movies. Well it takes two to make love, might as well I see what you see. He was stunned. Charming he says. I am single and live in Chantla. I thanked him for his invitation and say. I am with these three guys. We came together and we leave together. My companions looked the other way, hoping not to get red and wanted to melt into the ground. We walked home. Max and Tito are way behind me and Eric in the middle. Then they run ahead so we not together. Lots of eyes followed us. Once at home the boys are bragging. I only shook my head.

June 1st Monday morning Eric and his brother came early to me. Wound up and exited he tells me, if my our mom asks you, where we have been last night. I told her we've been in the park listening to Marimba music. As quickly as they came as quickly they left. I stood there in confusion. Not long after Martha came asking me. Where have you been last night? I told her I was with the boys in the park listening to marimba music. She knew I love the traditional music, but she didn't look very convinced. It was great music I said with passion. She left I was relieved, but not sure if she believed me. Mrs. Linda the elderly cook had lunch ready at twelve and it was my chore to bring it to the market for Martha and Augustine. Today I noticed almost every man smiling at me. I felt very uncomfortable. Some were especially friendly to me. They must all know. Early afternoon Martha and Augustine and I drive to the spring of Rio San Juan. A beautiful drive into the high mountains. The spring and beginning of the river has good earth. Corn and garlic grows especially good here. The garlic gets exported to south America. They loose no crops here, because there is always water. They build waterways to feed the fields. I is very green and once home to the guerillas, killing and assaulting many farmers. Now there are many homes and they wear their traditional clothes. Here is black skirts and a white blouse on the head a wrap with wool balls. I enjoy this. I take a picture of them. The old woman gets made and bends down to pick up stones ready to throw at me. Martha talks to her and explains to me. She doesn't like to be photographed. So we go on our way and take a farmer with us. Driving over the mother mountains. Sierra Madre. Another beautiful drive. I made Pizza for dinner, everybody loves it. Many times they asked me to stay and open a Pizza store. People would love it, you would be successful. I thought about it seriously. It was very tempting, but Ray and Nancy were waiting for me. And I hate to wash clothes by hand. I told them tomorrow I will be leaving. So we listened and recorded Marimba music from the radio where you can call in and request a song. The last song dedicated for me. I was surprised Augustin had called in and requested a song for me. I was very surprised and touched. By their kindness. Then Augustin talks about the married life and one day you may do it. Martha said unhappy tomorrow you leave, only god knows when you will possibly come back. It was very hard to leave these kind of people, but since the movie night I got to much attention and an excuse to leave. We knew that day would come. I wanted to leave before the parents found out. That evening we were all unhappy and wished I would stayed longer.

    June2nd Tuesday morning at six I left the house. It is overcast and cloudy everybody is depressed of my departure. They are like my parents to me. I loaded my bike and said good bye to everyone inclusive the dogs. Flako a nephew requests my scarf as a memory of me. Adios of to Mesilla. I pass through canyons, pass rivers with little water and towns were men stand guards with rifles. It feels uncomfortable and I think to myself just keep on driving. Its cold in the mountains. At the border the officers are friendly. Two quetzal for the bike and three quetzal for the tourist visa. It was easier to leave than enter the country.

Dr. Carlos (center) his sister, Martha, to his right his wife, Arciela, and nephews and cousins at the lake

Dr. Carlos and his wife, Arciela, and their kids on our outing in Guatemala

Guatemala mountains

A horse is used to carry the loads, bags, firewood, etc.

"Tikal" the big Mayan ruins in
Northern Guatemala

The roads to and from Tikal in the back country
in Guatemala

Mayan ruins Seibol in the rain forest

My motorcycle next to a giant tree.
Like an ant next to a giraffe

New land in the back country of Peten county

back country - the road to the beautiful river before Seibol

Martha and me at Mayan ruins

Eric's birthday (left of me) and his parents,
Augustin and Martha, along with guests

MEXICO

It was a cold morning. He filled out five papers for my bike, which took forever. The mountains covered with forests are so beautiful, with fabulous views. I looked down to the valley to a brown desert. A windy road going down with breath taking views. As I come down the mountain I start taking off my clothes. The valley is hot. In the afternoon I found a motel in Cintalapa. A nice clean place, the owners are very friendly. When I registered for the night, he told me. We passed you today in San Cristobal. A very nice green town. I was surprised, but didn't take the time to look around. What a coincidence. He asked where is Villarrica? In Paraguay. End of conversation. I took a warm shower my butt was swollen and covered with a heat rash. My body was in shock from cold to hot, even the night stayed hot, but I got a good night sleep.

June 3rd Wednesday I get up at five o'clock, pack my bike and continue driving, mostly through valleys with mountains in the background. Here they grow lots of mangoes as far the eye can see. Later on came as well pineapple fields, plums and sabote. At times I was tempted to stop and pick some fruit, but didn't take a chance. I get off the country road on to the Toll road. It costs 4 400 Pesos a lot of money for me. It was a good freeway from the valley leading up to the mountains. The road was straight as a candle. Happily driving thinking soon I am in America, when I suddenly had this vision. My rear tire passing me. Something was wrong, I could feel it. Driving in high speed I tried to come to a stop, because my rear was wiggling side to side and hard to keep straight and balanced. It took good

200 meters or more to stop. I got off the bike to look what is going on. My rear tire had gotten loose and is now stuck because of breaking. I was very upset and angry. I cleared my mind. What can I do? I have no tools. I looked around there is no home or town in sight. With great effort I put the bike on its stand. The rear tire was off the ground to take a closer look at the damage. The tire was jammed into the frame and brake. I tried to pull it out. No luck. Angry and frustrated I took a break and analyzed the problem and how to fix it. Some ideas came to me. It was very challenging and tuff to get the tire loose without the bike falling over. I managed to get the tire back in its place and the chain back on, but I need a nut to hold the tire. It took me a long time to get it done and I sweated like a pig. I took my coat off and the wind chilled my bones. I put my coat on and to get warm I started pushing the bike and the chain came loose and the tire came out. Now what? Here I am on a fast paced toll road to nowhere. In frustration I hold my thumb out in hope somebody will stop to help me. Many trucks and cars pass me. No one even considered to stop. I was upset. Did I look like a bum? Then I remembered people telling me. How some people pretend to have an accident. A person stops and gets assaulted or robbed. There was my luck. I had no hope. I saw a pickup coming and held my thumb out again. This one slowed down and stopped in a distance. What a surprise. Did the angels hear me? I wondered. I approach the pickup a man came out, I remembered him he remembers me. We met earlier at the pineapple stand. We were talking. He watched my bike while I went to the bathroom. I explained to him my scenario. He offers to take me to the next town. I was skeptical. He offered to put the bike in the back and pulled the tarp back. There sat a woman. I was relieved and agreed. I excused myself for a moment of my distrust a lot is happening. We loaded the bike and I sat close to the woman. We got covered up. The

truck gets back on the road a cold wind is blowing freezing my butt off. It seemed like a long drive to me. I imagined I had to walk it. The family took me till Puebla to a hotel restaurant " San Carlos" right along the road. I thanked the man for his help. The hotel owners were very nice and gave me a nice room and put the bike inside. I went to the restaurant I was the only guest there. A young girl came to take an order, give me a large soda, I wasn't hungry. The owner an old man and the young girl join me We sat for hours talking. Then the girl asks, when you get to America, will you settle and have a family? The old man shook his head and said calmly. No. when you make a trip like this, you never settle. You always will be traveling. The girl was in shock, asking lots of questions. She couldn't understand it. Every female wants to get married and have a family, she says. I was surprised by the old mans wisdom. We didn't know each other. I caught my breath and reinforced the old man, I will be always traveling. It is like a sickness. Our evening quieted down.

June 4th the old man and uncle to the hotel owners promised me to help. Every morning he goes to the market to shop and he would look for a nut. I waited all morning for him. I hung out with the son of the San Carlos Hotel. He spoke fluent English. He was living with his parents for many years in Los Angeles. They saved their money and returned home. Starting their own business. The son has his horses and they are happier and more relaxed. I had to agree with him. I loved his horses and to see him happy. The old man, his uncle showed up with the nut. He charged me a lot. Happily we put the nut on and fixed it. Now I was able to go downtown to get my speedometer fixed. Every mechanic referenced me to another. I got very frustrated. One young man accompanied me to a specialist for speedometer. He promised me to get it fixed. Skeptical I watched him work. It took him forever just to take it apart.

I was frustrated and the time passed. Finally he tells he can't fix it properly. It has a plastic wheel and he doesn't have the part. I was depressed waiting all this time for these news. He continued puttering and made the miles run backwards. That was better to nothing. His friends show up and went to lunch with him and smoked marihuana. I urged him, finish my bike first before you go. He asked me. Do you smoke? No, but why do you smoke? To feel good. To forget everyday life. I shook my head. No thanks I need a clear head. He left with his friends. I felt he did a partial job. The miles are running backwards, but the speedometer is working. I went to a bank to exchange some money. A fine dressed woman heard me and offers me to give me a better rate. The banker knew her and she lives close by, come to my house. I agreed to it. She has a VW bug her grown kids surround me. We all fit inside. It isn't far and we won't be long. So we squeeze in there like in a sardine can. She likes to help foreigners. Her daughter was an exchange student. They live in a beautiful house with an enclosed patio. They wanted me to stay all day with them, but I was concerned about my bike parked at the bank. So I took my money walked and back to the bank relieved. Everybody was asking me questions about Germany and the customs It was over whelming. I returned to the hotel and hung out with the neighbors that afternoon. To late to travel.

June 5th off to drive to San Luis de Paz about 550 kilometer away. In the morning I stopped at a fruit stand. The seller is in good spirits and upbeat. Offering a good variety of fruits. He tells me about shortcuts going north on country roads to avoid the boring expensive toll road. In Fresnillo a beige car passes me again. I've seen it before. The passenger holds his thumb up. I waved back. I found a motel for the night. I developed my pictures. I am very excited to be soon in America

June 6th excited I am back on the road. The back

road are not as good as the toll road. It was noon, when. I came close to a pickup truck parked off the road. Men were unloading things when I came closer they jumped off the rear and ran. I was scared and uncomfortable. I slowed down to look at them, but to scared to stop. What have they been stealing? When they realized I didn't stop they stopped running. I continued driving uneasy constantly looking in my rear mirror to see if they were coming. Nothing. Up the road came a gas station and general store I pulled into the parking lot. I sat there for a few minutes to see if the pickup would show up. Nothing. I wanted to buy a drink, but I didn't trust them. I continued my trip. That experience sat in my bones for a while. The scenery was boring mostly desert. In Durango I found a nice motel and put my bike inside. I heard music from a street festival. I followed the music it was already dark. Then I saw a food stand. They were cleaning the tables. Do you have food left? I asked. Just a little. That works for me, I said laughing. He gave me a plate, the salsa is on the table. I put some on it, fire came almost out of my mouth. He caught that. Is the salsa hot enough? He asks laughing. Its tolerable I joked back. I returned to my room to wash clothes. It was a warm night.

June 7th Sunday my goal was to make it today to Juarez the border town to America. Around nine o clock in the morning I stop at a stand. A group of people block my way. They were talking and I was trying to get through. Where are you going? asked one. I am going to America and that started a conversation. All of a sudden I was the center of attention. They were on the greyhound bus to Juarez everybody encouraged me to go with them on the bus. I told them frankly I have a motorcycle. Why should I ride the bus? Then you are not alone and have conversations with us. We put your bike in the bus, I have only ten passengers replies the bus driver. I was overwhelmed and found them to aggressive. Once again I told them I rather drive and took off without getting my beverage. Later I saw a cheese factory along the road in nowhere. I stop and go inside. I was amazed of how many cheeses they offered. A young woman came to ask what I wanted? I look around. She explains the cheeses then she asked where are you from. Germany, but now from Paraguay. She got so excited she ran in the back to get her father He came out and shook my hand and we talked. They were excited that I am from Germany and drove my bike to America. They would a have kept me all day. Finally I got my cheese and went back on the road. They were so happy to see me. What an unusual way to buy cheese. When I ate my cheese it was so good, I wished I had bought more. Due to the heat I bought a small amount. After lunchtime I left the a city when I hear a horn blowing. I move more to the right. There was the horn again. Angry I turn around to see the greyhound bus was next to me. The passengers are waving at me. I waved back. The bus took off. We did it in the same time. I felt good. I was glad not to be on the bus. They would a drive me insane with all their questions. As I came closer to Chihuahua I thought I reached the moon. A boring drive and many dead dogs along the road. It is heart breaking to see how reckless they are while driving. A lonely farmer is plowing the field with a horse followed by a dog. I thought be careful dog stay off the road. These drivers have no mercy. In the afternoon the last city before Juarez I leave the town I hear a horn blowing. I move over and the horn blows again and again. It wouldn't stop so I look over my shoulder. I see the greyhound bus next to me. All the passengers hanging out the window shouting of joy and waving to me. I wave back. We were all excited and surprised. I smiled. The bus speeded off. I stayed back to avoid breathing the exhaust. The sky got dark, the bus got smaller and smaller. Worried I looked at the sky while driving faster and faster trying to escape the clouds.

Instead it got darker and darker in the desert. Thunder and lightening added to my tension on a straight road. I look down to see how fast I am going to notice the fuel idle is in red. I hoped to make it in time to a gas station. My eyes fixed on the road hoping to see one. The beige car passed me up again. He waved this time. It got even darker and a cold wind was blowing and light rain. Nervous and angry I wished I would a have been on the bus warm and dry. There in a distance in nowhere it seems there is a station. I wasn't sure between the dark clouds and the monotone desert, it blended in. I fixed my eyes on that spot. Hoped and prayed to make it. The closer I came I realized it wasn't my imagination. Here in this god forsaken place. With my last drop of gas I pull into the station. There was that beige car again filling his gas as well. Tired and exhausted I park and fill up my tank. He comes over and we talk. We are passing each other now for three days. Are you from Costa Rica? No, Paraguay. They looked at my license plate. Our conversation had ended and they walked away. I pay for my gas. We continued our trip without speaking another word to each other. The weather was bad almost till Juarez. The outskirts had nice motels, but I wanted to be close to the border. So in the morning I can spend my last pesos and cross the border. Downtown is dirty and I had a hard time to find a motel with my bike. One was upstairs. The men were friendly and helped me carry my bike upstairs, we left it in the hallway. Everyone was friendly, but the room was filthy. My room was above a disco. Across was a street café where I got some food. That night I slept fully clothed in bed, afraid to catch something.

June 8th it had rained Sunday night and the streets are wet. I went to the dollar market and bought a t shirt of good quality and then searched for a Honda dealership. After several inquiries one man admitted, there is none. Disappointed, I bought some tortillas and oranges with my last pesos. I returned to the motel to load my bike and drive to the border. I was very excited. There was lots of traffic. A long line of cars wanting to cross the bridge to the border. I drove in between the cars. One car was blocking my way, politely I said excuse me. Nothing. I blowed my horn nothing. Again nothing. Then I yell at them. Get out of my way. All of a sudden the girl takes her feet off the dashboard and the driver pulls over with their loud music. I passed and thanked them.

AMERICA

Over the bridge to custom # two. A black officer demanded to open all my bags. He searched them all and found my oranges. You can't bring them into the country. I protested I just bought them. He says you can eat them inside the immigration building but move your bike first to station # five. I did, then I walked through a long tunnel to get to the immigration building. It was a huge room with a large crowd of people. Mostly dark skinned people, I stuck out like a sore thumb. I stand in line while eating my oranges. There were may be three people ahead off me. I handed the officer my passport. He asked me a few questions. One officer spoke to me in German, which really helped me a lot. Are you the one with the motorcycle? Yes, I said surprised. He handed me a white card, fill it out. Your destination, address. I asked him for a six month visa. He looked through my passport. Pages and pages including the last page full of stamps. He told me to wait. I waited and waited hoped he didn't go to lunch. After a long wait, he returned. I was so relieved when he came back. He handed my closed passport to me. Nervous I asked him. Did you give me six months? Calmly the officer replies. One year! I almost shouted from joy my eyes got big from happiness. I thanked him. In joy I run and jumped through the building back to my bike. All the Mexican looked at me. They thought I was crazy or lost my mind. As fast I could I run back to my bike to station five. Excited I took my bike off to downtown looking for a tourist office to get a map. It was free. What a surprise. It was a surprise to me that people avoided me. There getting out of my way.

Why, because of my motorcycle helmet? I needed to find a Honda dealership, so I went back to the tourist office. It is all the way out in Montana, a district of El Paso. The roads are big and wide so clean. I noticed as well Americans are now driving smaller cars. Just a few years ago everybody had a big huge vehicle. I miss that. There came the Honda dealership. A huge place lots of motorcycle are on display. They are all so big compared to mine. I was impressed. I walk into the showroom a traditional biker approached me. Can I help you? Yes I need battery acid. We walk together through the big showroom half way the biker says. You need a new battery and I smell Mexican gasoline. I was impressed. How do you know that? He explained that Mexican gas is of low grade and my battery is done. Wow I thought my mechanics in Paraguay thought I could make it till Bolivia instead I made it with my bad battery until America. Always filling up the acid. The biker Mr. Rat looks at my license. Where is Villaricca? In Paraguay. He was stunned. He looks over my bike and told me, you need a few things done. He gives me a 20 % discount. I was very happy about that. Mr. rat filled my battery with water and acid. They had to order a new one for me. We got into a conversation and he invited me to his biker bar tonight. I was excited. Sure I will come and looked foreword to meet more bikers. For the parts they send me to F & M cycle, ask for Mike. On the other side of town. I did. I needed a speedometer. He had a used one. A German man helped to put it on. How much is it? Nothing. I was touched of their kindness. While we worked Mr. Rat came. Why didn't you wait for me? I felt at home. Aren't you working? You can go away like that? I didn't understand it. The guys talked. We help each other I have one year visa in the states. It felt like a dream. We return to the Honda dealership. Mr. Rat changed the oil. From here we go to open his biker bar. Which is huge. To the left is the bar and to the right in a corner a stage for bands and dancing. The whole wall there is covered with pictures. Bikers, girls topless, wild parties. Wow I was over whelmed. We stood there for a while looking and chatting. It was a different world. We go to the bar and have a drink as customers pour in. Mr. Rat tells them about my trip.

They are impressed. From Paraguay on a little bike. That's amazing. One guy gives me the address from the international biker club. To have contacts when you travel. I thanked him for his thought fullness. I was the talk of the night. Later on Mr. Rat warned me of girls liken girls. I came from the bathroom and a girl hit on me. I didn't understand what she wanted. Luckily he intervened and asked me to go behind the counter and told her, I am not interested in girls. I was glad when she left. We had a sausage with sauerkraut. That was good. It was a quiet night, not many customers. It rained outside. He closed the bar early and went to get his car. I was glad not to stay on a campground as planned. It was far from here. He offered his hide a bed. He lives in a small apartment with an old fat cat. Don't you lock your car? I asked him. He waved, no one bothers. I watched TV while Mr. Rat cooked dinner. Steak, potato balls and peas. It was a good time.

June 9th in the morning. He made coffee. He gives me a U.S. mailbag to pack my luggage. This is much easier than three. He had worked as a mailman in the past. He gave me as well two Harley Davidson T-shirts. He squares me up, he said. I thank him for everything. Then he drove me to the Honda Dealer. My bike wasn't ready, the mechanics were still working. The parts came late. The young manager invited me to coffee and biscuits. The sales manager joined us. He said it's better to get your bike fixed. it's a long drive to California. The manager paid for the work. Tell this over F & M cycle and we all laughed. I was glad they got the parts and the work done. Finally at eleven in the morning. I caught the highway to "Las Cruces." I was so happy. My joy for driving on this big nice road didn't lasted to long. Every time a big truck passed, I was pulled with them. The strong wind battered me around. I felt like a leaf in the wind. A biker passed me and waved. That felt great. It will be a long nerve wrecking drive west. Later I stopped at a rest area. Something was wrong with the bike. I looked it over and saw I lost the nut for the stabilizer of the frame. I got mad, not again. Fast I caught my anger brought it under control. I looked around and saw a maintenance man cleaning. I approached him. Do you possibly have a nut for that size? Pointing at my bike. He scratches his head. May be, we normally don't have those things around. I encouraged him to look. I followed him to his maintenance room. He searched and searched, nothing. Disappointed I return to my bike. In the meantime two pickups with a Harley Davidson on the back had arrived. I stare at the biker, he stared back. Then the maintenance man came with a nut. The biker approaches us. Looking at what was going on. The nut fits. It may not last long explained the maintenance man. I thought about going on country roads to California. The freeway scared me. The biker said, lets ask the owner if he gives you a lift. An old black man without a shirt and shoes approached us. The biker introduced him to us. I was shocked. And asked him if he could give me a lift to the next town. He asked me. Where are you going? To California, he says me too. To Anaheim, come with us. With mixed feelings I agreed. The old man drove the pickup and the young biker and I we drove the pickup in tow. We loaded my bike next to the Harley. It was a long boring drive through the desert in Texas and Arizona. In the evening we stopped at a Mac Donald, the old man says get yourself something to eat. There was nothing I liked and ate instead my tortillas. We drove into the night then pulled into a rest area. The old man came to tell us, we are staying here for the night. It was a warm night. I was surprised where are we sleeping? I will sleep in my truck says the old man and walked away. The biker actually a hitch hiker got picked up from the old man. He needed a driver to tow his broken pickup back to California. He was a nice person, but looked like a homeless man and it was hard to believe that he owned all that. Something is not right. The young man responded you watch to much TV. I haven't except last night. So what are we doing now? He said charming, getting closer to me. He stunk like a Billy goat. I wondered when he took a shower last. We talked a little more, I wasn't going to sleep with him in the cabin. Where will you sleep? I told him firm I will be sleeping on top of the toolbox in the back of the truck. It will be cold. You won't feel it. Thank you for your concerns.He thought I am crazy and just joking. I opened the door and climbed on the back. I put my beach towel down on the toolbox. My luggage was my pillow and my leather coat my blanket. The night went fast. I awoke it was cool and fresh. Soon the old man came to tell us we continue I was very happy. I rode a while with the old man and then later the young man drove with him to give him a break driving. I never trusted any of them. We stopped for breakfast. The old man invited us pulling a big bundle of money out of his dirty pants. Order what you want. I had a real breakfast. Hash browns, eggs and bacon, so did the old man. The young man had French toast. It was very good. The old man asked me to drive with him for a while. I asked him. Why you look so shabby? I have been on the road a few days. My truck broke down, so I went home to Los Angles to get this one. I felt a little better now. Through Phoenix it was a very hot. When we reached California the young man rode with the old man I drove the pickup in tow. They were talking intensively. Finally we reached the outskirts of Los Angles, it was afternoon. So happy to be here so close to San Francisco now. We drove through a poorer neighborhood and stopped in front of two Victorian houses. The black neighbor woman stood at her front door with a fat cigar in her mouth. Rolling that cigar around in her mouth probably thinking. His wife is not home and he brings a chick home. Her dogs barked at us in the fenced yard. I was very uncomfortable and agreed with her, without saying a word just by looking at her. I asked the old man before he backed up into his driveway. Let's unload my bike. He said later. Why not now. Relax for a while before you continue. The young man directed him backing the pickups into his driveway. I was very uncomfortable, but had no choice. We go into the big house and tells me to make myself comfortable in the living room. He excused himself and went upstairs to take a shower. Here I stood alone in this huge living room wondering. Where is the young man? All a sudden he was gone. The old man came back clean and shiny. I asked him if I could call Ray. He gave me the telephone. Ray was on his way out and asked for the phone number. I told him I would stay the night and continue tomorrow. Ray promised to call back later. Where is the young man I asked. I sent him over to my sons house to get some drugs. I got more uncomfortable. The old man encouraged me to take a shower. I didn't care for. Finally he says follow me upstairs. I did, and he had filled the bathtub with hot water and some strong soap. He tells me to take a bath and closed the door behind him. The strong smell irritated my sinus. At the sink stood a bottle. It read Pine sol all purpose cleaner. I was shocked. He must think I haven't bathed in weeks like him. I let the water out and go down stairs. The old man lays on one couch in his shorts. He encourages me to sit down. I sit on the opposite couch of him across the large living room. It was silent. All a sudden he pulled his penis out of the pants Then he asks me to make love to him. I protested. He says calmly if you don't do it voluntary I will force you and pulled a large revolver from under his pillow and pointed it at me. Fear went through my body, what should I do? I have to get close enough to him and kick the gun out of his hand. Calmly I jumped on my feet, looking him in the eyes. In a firm tone I tell him. It doesn't work that way, put your gun away while walking slowly toward him. Half way across the room he got up and said I will put it away. He passed me to put his revolver on top of a huge cabinet. I was so relieved. I run to the front door the a storm door was locked. Fear and anger went through my body. I will jump with a sidekick through a window I looked thru every window and everywhere two Rotweiler dogs greeted me with fleshing teeth. The only safe way is the front door. Very upset I returned to the living room. He sat there smiling you can't get out. I demanded from him to open the door or I will jump through it. You want to save yourself the repair open the door now. He felt my anger and knew I wasn't kidding. Casually he got up and unlocked the door. Sarcastic he says, but you can't get your bike out. He parked to close to the house. It was very tight. I grabbed my bag and told him. Let that be my problem. I dashed outside put my bags next to the pickup and tried to lift my bike over a six foot chain link fence topped with bob wires and there was a gap between the truck and the fence. I realized I couldn't do it alone I need somebody on the other side of the fence to hold the bike up. I went to speak to his neighbor. A black guy hanging out with a couple girls. He whined if the neighbor doesn't help he wouldn't help. The neighbor would later come after him. Angry I walked away. I stopped an ice cream truck coming down the street. In Spanish he told me he is afraid. Nobody has guts here. I walked away from him, he speeded off. A couple houses down I saw a two young men working. In Spanish I asked them for help to unload my bike off the pickup. Happily they came. We found out it was easier said than done. I let them on the truck while I stood by the fence receiving the front tire over the fence. The black guy came complaining I would ruin his yard. I told him help me or get out of my way. He complained like a champion.I just ignored him and spoke only Spanish with my helpers. It was very hard work and took lots of coordination. Two thirds of the bike was sitting on the fence. It was getting to heavy for me. The Spanish helper took my place and I went on the pickup to lift the rear over the fence. The old man came out complaining we are ruining his fence. I yelled at him its your own fault. I almost fell on the fence for not paying attention. I focused as we lifted the bike higher to get the rear tire over. I needed to sit the bike on the bob wire to go and help the receivers. The tall black man and his ladies yelled and surrounded us and trying to interfere with us. By accident I stood on his foot and almost fell. Angrily I yelled at him. Go away. Leave us alone. All three of us managed to get the bike over the fence. Relieved and soaked in sweat we sat the bike on the ground and pushed it on the sidewalk. The blacks were all speechless and went inside their houses. I ran to get my bag and thanked my helpers a thousand times. They just laughed and were happy to help me. I didn't waste time to leave not knowing if the old man calls his son or buddies to send someone for revenge. Afraid and scared I drove west searching for the freeway. The residential turned into businesses with high traffic and lots of people. It was like an ant house. At a parts store I parked and asked people for directions. Most of them where Hispanic, they didn't know how to get to the freeway. It was a huge store, people everywhere and groups of people standing together talking. I asked several times for directions. Most of them just ignored me or didn't know. Finally one white American broke away from a group and explained the directions. I was so nervous and shaking, I asked three times to retain the info. Patiently he explained it again and I thanked him several times and hit the road. The traffic was very busy and I managed to see the freeway sign and drove up the ramp in a half circle. The freeway was a parking lot bumper to bumper. Easily I drove between the cars. Just before going on the freeway I see the sign San Diego! I was mad. That's the wrong way so I squeeze in between the cars, but one Asian lady blocked the way. She looked at me scared. Could you please move I am on the wrong freeway. She happily moved. I drove against traffic down the ramp. Back on the street I see the sign for San Francisco. Happily I drive on the long onramp. Then the road had grooves and my bike vibrated. Scared I slowed down afraid to fall, I felt a like ropedancer on a bike. The onramp went on forever, I noticed in my rear view mirror as I held up traffic. The single lane entered the freeway and many cars passed me at a high speed. A red pickup passed me a male passenger held his arm out of the window and yelled at me from the top of his lungs" Asshole" I didn't blame him. The camper from Oregon passed me up. We met at the gas station before entering the freeway. They must think I am cuckoo. I drove only 40 miles an hour. I met them at the gas station and asked them if I could follow them and stay the night next to their camper. I had told them briefly my incident. He looked at me like a ghost. They passed me and I felt alright on the freeway north finally. Later the traffic slowed down, to stop and go, but nothing said San Francisco. I got concerned is this the right way? I tried to ask a couple of slow moving cars one right after the other. When I approached them they rolled up their window or pulled away. So I ventured out driving in between the cars all over the five lane freeway. I spotted a Latino driver and asked him in Spanish for the way. He didn't know. He looked afraid and tried to get away. I asked another question, he didn't know either. Angrily I asked him, do you know your name? he shook his head. Frustrated I continued driving in between cars in rush hour. It looked like a slow moving parking lot. There I spotted a beige convertible Mercedes. I drove next to him in the middle lane, asking him the way to San Francisco. He smiled and said just look for " Golden State" pointing at the sign ahead. Just then the traffic picked up, before I could ask another question. He speeded off pointing straight ahead to the sign and waved. I waved back. I couldn't follow him as fast. He was the only smiling driver on the road. Traffic picked up fast, cars drove around me and cut me off. I knew I had to get over to the slow lane. Crossing the lanes was a challenge. Everybody was in a hurry. Due to drafts and wind I get only 40-45 miles per hour. I drove through the city and up the mountain. The plateau was so beautiful. I love it here, but I hated these big trucks and the double trailers. Their draft whipped me around like a leaf in the wind. The beautiful scenery made up for it. It was getting dark and I was still driving. Wondering where could I stay the night? Coming off the mountain I read a sign "campground" I took that exit and followed the sign. Everything was closed. So I rung the night bell at the office. A friendly person showed up. I asked for a space and my bike. You have a tent he asked? I nodded. He gave me a space number. Its ten dollar for the night. I found it, the numbers are lightened up. Next to a wooden table with benches on both sides. Here I stood in a chilly, damp night I got hungry and opened my can of pork and beans which I bought in El Paso. The food didn't taste good cold. I remembered I still had kerosene left from Paraguay, but my little stove is gone. What should I do? I found an empty sardine can in the trash. I poured kerosene in it. I poured the beans in my metal cup and occasionally stirred. I stood shivering waiting for the beans to get warm. Thinking to myself. It's ok to look stupid, but don't be stupid. After I ate I wondered where should I sleep? The bench was to narrow. I tried the table. It was to damp and cold. This will be a long night, I said to my self. I couldn't get comfortable and I needed to use the bathroom. I opened the door, it was warm and cozy in there. May be I'll just stay here the night. I returned to my bike and packed everything and pushed the bike inside the bathroom. Next to my bike I put my beach towel on the floor. Leaving enough room for others to use the toilets. My bag became my pillow and with my coat on I slept on the floor. A few times ladies came in to use the bathroom. They made comments, but I ignored them and pretended to sleep. With sunrise I got up. I was back on the road again. I continued driving on highway Five north. Exited I took 101 north through the valley. This turned into a really nice drive. Farms and orchards just gorgeous, breathtaking I love it here. I stopped at a fruit stand next to the road to buy fresh apricots, peaches and cherries. They tasted so good. I continued later to take Freeway 280. Exited at the rest area with a priest monument I stopped to call Ray collect. You are only five minutes from our house, he gave me directions and saying. I won't be home, but Nancy will be waiting for you. I asked a man to take a picture of me on my motorcycle before continuing. He didn't mind. I thanked him. I was back on the freeway taking the next exit. It was a beautiful area on top of a mountain ridge. The houses and lots are bigger here. Another turn and I drive into their half circle driveway. I turned off my engine. Nancy came smiling to the front door. Holding her arms out. You made it. Welcome to California. She has that hearty smile and gave me a big hug. She went to work and Andrea from Austria visited with me. Ray and Nancy took me everywhere and I met many of their friends. They were very good to me. They all wished I could speak fluent English to tell my story. I talked in broken English, some Spanish and some German with them and we got along just fine. Ray had a huge video collection and showed me the Spanish movie " El Norte." I could relate to the movie. I have been to the Guatemala mountains. After three weeks I moved to a doctors house. She had cancer and went through chemotherapy and needed help. I became their housekeeper in exchange for room and board. Their Collie became my best friend. Six weeks later I was driving on the freeway and the police stopped me. He asked me for my license and gave me a ticket, for not registering my bike and for driving on the freeway. It must be a 150 cc or a bigger bike. He told me after four weeks in the states you will have to transfer your registration to California. I told Ray and Nancy their good friend Andrea from Austria worked as police officer. She explained to me that you go to the DMV and register your bike and get a California drivers license and transfer your bike. The judge will void your ticket. I did the written test in Spanish and I passed. Then I took the driver test. He told me to drive in a circle. That was very easy for me. I have experiences now. I didn't when I went on my trip. That's how I became a Californian.

    I discovered a Tae-kwon-do-club and joined. I became friends with Iva Georges and we motivated each other to train. On the weekends the doctor let me use their older car to drive to motorcycle Poker Runs. The idea was to meet other bikers make friends and see more of California. At the Poker runs everybody has to sign in and I would ask for a ride for the run. It was fun and a good experience. For the first run I called for directions and inquired what is a poker run. She explained it in detail. I told then the lady briefly about my trip. On a 125Honda from Paraguay to San Francisco, approximately 11 000 miles one way. At the end of the run the Pacer Motorcycle Club in Solana gave me a trophy" International Rider 1987." many bikers were impressed others said. They would've have done it on a bigger bike. Others wished I could tell my stories. I met lots of good people and saw California's back roads. Later my travel boots carried me to Texas visiting Mr. Rat and his mom. I also went to Maui, Hawaii to Ray and Nancy's new home. In 1989 I went to Paraguay, visiting my friends and they told me stay in America, because of the political unrest. President Stroessner got overthrown. I went to Colombia to see Dorothy, Capt. Uribe and Jaco. What a happy reunion it was. In 1990 I traveled throughout Brazil and Paraguay with my friend Renate from Germany. I got married to Gordon Anderson. He ran a public computer bulletin board. He was known as " Toad Hall" and his home was his castle. In 1992 I traveled to New Zealand. His mom Shirley married an old high school friend a few months later. Two widowers and lovebirds. Paul Petersen was a self made millionaire born in Denmark. He was always joking, I liked him a lot. Shirley and I tolerated each other. I worked for them twice a week in their Atherton home. One morning Paul told me, Shirley doesn't want him to buy that new Mercedes. I looked him in the eyes and asked him. What color are you getting?

Shirley gave me that look. If eyes could kill I would a been dead. A few weeks prior Paul had told me. That governor Wilson implemented the luxury tax and a new car would cost now 125 000$. I told him, write acheck. He had to laugh and a few days later the new 500SEL Mercedes was parked in the garage. In 1992 I met A.J. a writer and consultant. I told him about my trip and let him read the beginning of my book" With a parrot through South America" He gave me his harsh professional critic as expected. As well did Laurie Harper a publisher. We meet at the store" Time for a book." One day a man approached me. Can you read old German? Yes, I said. He had a hand written letter from Albert Einstein to a friend. He had high hopes it contained a formula. I immediately knew it wouldn't. We agreed to meet over a cup of coffee. I translated the letter written in the early1940's in Switzerland. No formula. He was disappointed, not me, but he was impressed how easily I had read and translated the letter. Albert writes at the end. I give a shit in the hectic of time. I just live my life and think and think. In spring Sally, Gordon's younger sister living in San Diego got married in Atherton. Everybody was uptight for the rehearsal night. I told Marla, Clarks wife and Gordon's brother let's rock the boat tonight and shake them up. I showed up at church with Pink hair and a red shoe and a blue shoe. The older guests gave me all dirty looks, but Paul only smiled. Over cocktails Sally's friends told me. Don't worry we just haven't left L.A. (Los Angles) I felt good. Mission accomplished. In 1993 I went to visit my friends in Paraguay and Bolivia. I returned very sick. Still weak and training for six years I took the black belt test and failed. We got divorced. I just asked for his signature and to be free. I moved to Bolivia, but life wasn't so simple anymore. I felt like an exotic animal, always guarded and protected. It took me a long time to get well. Willy Ordonez saw in me a trophy wife. That's not me, but he insisted to get married anyway. A good year later in 1994 we came to America. We stayed with my friends Fred and Ursula Hackenberg. Thanks to Dr. Stewart my health improved and I got on my feet again. In 1995 we had our first son Wolfgang. My father was so happy to be grandpa and even happier the boy was named after him. He sent me money to stay home with him, instead of going back to work after six weeks. We were close and we both traveled the world independently. Through me he saw Paraguay, Brazil and America. My father was on a tour on the west coast ending in San Francisco. My mom stayed home due to an emergency operation. A year later my parents took a cruise from Panama to Mexico. I went to visit them for few days in Ensenada, Mexico. Sadly my father only saw his grandson on pictures. He died five weeks later. We flew to

Germany to attend the funeral. In 1996 my mom visited us for an extended time to help and being with her grandson. Our second son Friedrich was born in 1997 and named him after my fathers middle name and my mom's dad. My Mom visited again to help and raise her grandkids. We traveled extensively together. Thanks to Dino Fry my ex and I became mutual friends. He helped me with computer problems. Later he built a computer with children programs for my kids. I was extremely grateful, but not Willy. Wolfgang became so good, that he later taught me computer skills. In 1999 the boys and I flew to Germany to attend my brothers wedding. With my mom we toured Germany and Austria visiting friends and family. Both boys attended the German Kindergarten in Menlo Park. In 2000 my mom visited us again and together we all flew to Lima, Peru on to Bolivia visiting with Willy and his family. Against his will, my mom, the boys and I took the bus through the Chaco to Paraguay visiting my friends. Instead of a 24 hour drive it took three nights and two days, because the overloaded bus broke a few times in the desert with limited food and water. We arrived at my friends house filthy, hungry and thirsty. They understood and were glad to see us. Most important we saw Ramona. She was very ill. Two months later she passed away. I was very happy we made that trip, but Willy was furious that we spent only a few days with him and his family in Camiri, Bolivia. I reminded him. We are not trophies to be shown off and it wasn't my fault the bus broke down. My mom will never forget that drive and for her age she handled it very well. All the Bolivians respected her for that. In 2001 Judy a friend, the boys and I went to St. Paul, Minnesota. We both were distributors for Ecoquest and attended the convention. Wolfgang was old enough to go with Bill Converse the owner and founder of the company and other kids on a science tour while the adults were learning. Friedrich was in daycare. In 2002 one weekend the three of us visited Ed and Judy in Groveland. To the boys joy it snowed overnight. Friedrich and Judy were buddies. Judy had a sledge for them. They have their birthdays on the same day. While there Ed and I went shopping to buy a fixer upper home. Judy laughed, putting me and Ed together is dangerous. We would buy up the whole area. When I broke the news to Willy. He said, are you out of your mind? We moved to Mariposa. He loves the city. I love the country. At first he said he would move, but he changed his mind. He continued working in the city and came on the weekends to pester us with his negative vibes. In 2003 the boys and I went to New Orleans Louisiana, the yearly Ecoquest Convention. The kids toured the town while the adults were learning. In Mariposa the boys played soccer, baseball, and 4H and Sunday to church. In 2004 my mom visited us and we traveled locally. Several times to Yosemite Park and beyond. With my kids I raised goats, sheep, pigs, chicken, geese, duck, turkey and my Macaws were in the backyard. We had our own meat, eggs, milk and cheese. I home schooled, made home improvements and managed our rental properties. In my spare time I worked with Ecoquest selling Air purifiers. That's how we met Joyce and Bob. We became friends. A year later they bought a house in Le Grand. Joyce rescues Cockatoos Parrots and Bob decided to become a farmer and rescued a goat " Roger " from my stewpot. The boys called them Grandma and Grandpa. Roger needed a companion, so Joyce and I went to an auction in the valley to buy a companion. It was 100 degrees in the shade. We ended up buying two goats and two sheep. We called Bob to bring the van, because they wouldn't fit in my 230E Mercedes. Bob had a fit. You told me one not four. I calmed Bob down. Just be glad. I didn't buy the nearly 1 000 lb feral sow for 9.53 $ and butcher her in that heat in your backyard. Bob was glad I didn't. In December of 2005 we bought our fourth property.

My dream 20 acres on top of a mountain with three small homes. A huge bolder close by gave a 360 degree view to Yosemite and beyond.

My goats herds love to rest on the granite bolder. My tenant Randy and I often sat there and looked at the sunset. Randy helped out a lot. I thought this was my last move until I died, so did Randy. Every march is the storytelling festival in Mariposa. We drove to town in the evening to attend a storytelling. When we came out about eight inches or more of snow had fallen. The boys were delighted, but we had to drive home. A long hill up on highway 41. People predicted, you are not going to make it in that Mercedes. I told the boys to get in. The roads were not plowed. It was a chaos many people were frustrated or stuck. Cars parked along the street. We passed everyone in the night fishtailing up the long hill. Finally we turned on our dirt road. At the pond we couldn't make it up the hill. We parked the car and started walking in the snow. The moon was so bright and the stars lit up the road. It was silence and peaceful everything was white. We were full of joy and happiness. The boys and I looked to the moon and thanked him for the light to lead us home. It was less than a mile to walk. To us it was Christmas in march. I never forgot that night, like out of a storybook. In the summer of 2006 Wolfgang showed the second year a goat for 4H at the County Fair. He won first Prize in showman ship for his goat. He got a big trophy and a belt buckle with a goat on it. All his rabbits won ribbons. I was proud of him. Friedrich hung out with the kids. He wasn't old enough to show at 4H. Willy disapproved of everything what I and the kids did and disagreed with our rural lifestyle. He wanted a divorce for years and told the Pastor at counseling. You are my witness. I want a divorce. I don't care about my wife. I don't care about my kids or the properties. I want to be free. The Pastor said to me. Go home and talk to him. I smiled and said I have been talking for 11years. It's over. You heard him. Three weeks later on October 2006 I granted his wish and filed for divorce.

I asked my tenant and friend Jim. A wonderful person and caring, if he could help me with the paperwork. He was seeking a quiet place to live and grieve over the death of his wife. Looking back it was the wrong thing to do. Willy got served and as thank you he tried to burn the house with me and the boys. Blaming Jim for our divorce. He wasn't looking for a relationship nor did I. My friend Judy volunteered to write a letter for the court. (Enclosed) In the evenings Jim came over and sometimes Randy socializing. We had no TV, only Videos.

The boys loved Jim and Friedrich did his homework in no time. We sat for hours at the dinner table talking and laughing. Sometimes we went for a drive to Yosemite, Bass lake. He let the boys drive their small motorcycle after work was done. The boys enjoyed to have a positive Adult male around and interacting with them The boys played Rambo, they built a tent in the front lawn pretending to be on a military missions. Exploring the property going through the brush and at night only be covered in rash from poison oak. Willy had visitation and heard all the good news and he kept the kids. Willy's action and behavior destroyed many people's dreams and hopes. I sold my goats, the fox and coyotes ate all my chickens. All the properties got sold, due to Willy's request and all the tenants had to move involuntarily. His action brought together and in 2007 Jim and I moved to southern California. After filing for my divorce I easily passed my Real Estate Test. I got my Real Estate Sales license and trained with Century 21 Award and got a listing. In the summer we went to Cabo, Mexico In 2008 we visited Ray and Nancy in Maui, Hawaii. They inspired me to finally write my travel story, while working part time for CDS as sales advisor at sought after Costco. In 2009 my mom planned to have the whole family together and celebrate her 80th birthday. Willy wouldn't allow the boys to go with me to Germany. It was a huge disappointment for my mother. She had everything planned. My mom and I spent three weeks of quality time visiting families and touring. In 2010 Ray passed away, luckily we saw him a couple of weeks prior. Yes, we always will be traveling.

Rest area on freeway 280 near Hillsborough

My old license plate from Paraguay "Villarrica" before getting Californian license plate

Nancy and dog, Trixie, in their home in Hillsborough, California in 1987

Ray and Nancy in Maui, Hawaii 1988 on the beach while I visited

Visiting Nancy and Ray in Maui, Hawaii in 2008

Jim and I in Maui

www.ingramcontent.com/pod-product-compliance
Lightning Source LLC
Chambersburg PA
CBHW031639040426
42453CB00006B/149